Fed Up?
Changed Up!
Now What?

Truths for Dating, Marriage, and Rape Prevention

By Teaira & Greg Curry

Why I Wrote This Book

When it comes to marriage, people often focus on the wedding. We see the lights, the cameras with all the photos, and we often stop there. I did, but that's a wedding. This book challenges us to build a marriage.

You may wonder, "How does a marriage stay healthy and filled with light when I can't even get past dating!" I asked myself these exact questions while on my quest to find love and if anyone ever tells you relationships are a walk in the park, you may want to consider having another conversation with them or someone else who has been married for a great length of time.

In this transparent book, I'll share my personal journey of dating. At age 18, I quickly transitioned from a sheltered teen in foster care to a wild, promiscuous, love-seeking party animal. Before I received a wedding ring, I dated a drug dealer, strippers, maniacs, B-list celebrities, and I even tried my hand at committing to my best friend. The 'fast life' came to a violent crawl when I dated a Jamaican rapist. The rape setup and medical diagnosis that resulted from the assault made me see that I had to slow down and reevaluate my worth as a woman and as a potential wife.

Once I became a married woman with the man of my dreams, I discovered I was clueless as to what it meant to be a life-partner. As a young couple we had no idea of the maintenance a marriage required. As a woman, I focused more on the wedding and neglected the marital part of things. As a man, my husband initially focused on becoming the breadwinner and leader of the family by carrying all of our burdens. Initially, we had no understanding about the love, respect, communication, prayer, dedication, and the endurance that would be required of us. We were rudely awakened by reality.

Our transition from living the single life to a life of marriage was definitely not easy. We decided to be as candid as possible while sharing our stories with you. It is our hope that sharing our truths will create better relationship outcomes. If you are on your journey of love right now and it's rocky, don't lose hope. There is someone out there that will treat you like the true King/Queen you are no matter how dirty your past may be.

If your perception of partnership is clouded, you will gain clarity while reading this book. Ask yourself, are you really fed up? If so it's time to Change up! If you already have 'Changed up' where do you go from here?

Dedication

First, I dedicate this book to God, because without Him there would be no book. He provided us with wisdom when we had no clues. He sent resources when we seemingly had nothing left, love when there was a void, strength when there were no muscles in my spiritual body, confidence when I felt like a failure, peace when all hell broke loose, and He replaced my bucket of tears with an ocean of joy. After I wrote this book, I thought I was done, but God communicated it's not just a book, it's a movement.

Next, thank you to my loving husband, who found salvation through the midst of our troubles. When God became the head of our lives, it was as if we had renewed our love and our vows.

To my precious children, I love all of you. Each one of you brought me closer to my purpose and gave me a reason to keep going when I had nothing left. I knew I had to improve my ways to be the best example I could be to you.

Last, but not least, to everyone who supported the 'Changed Up, Now What?' movement. By purchasing a book, being a guest on my podcast show, praying for us, donating, or sending an encouraging word, you are appreciated and for that I love you.

If I were to write the names of every contributor, I would need to create another book! Know that if you have ever done anything for us, you are appreciated.

Table of Contents

Introduction

When it comes to dating, I've made plenty of mistakes. Although I'm a Christian, don't look at me as perfect, because I'm not, I will always be grateful I'm forgiven. All I wanted to do was live life, have fun and find someone special to share my life with. Once I turned 18, free to make my own decisions, I discovered the consequences of not valuing myself.

If you're reading my book, please know I love you. I love you enough to put all of my personal business out there for your personal gain. These stories are not intended to bash men, but rather to share how a life without Christ, and His purpose can go so wrong. If everyone was born with a public camera attached to their hip, we'd see some shameful things on our lists. Recorded will be things we regret, shameful things, and actions that simply waste time and life. BUT, I'm thankful for the hardships I experienced in order to learn the lessons that taught me the value of myself and an understanding of how to treat my spouse.

I had to get sick of being treated like someone's second best trash to understand that I was the one throwing my own value away. I destroyed myself every time I said yes to someone that clearly said no to me. Their actions spoke loud and clear, but the truth was drowned out in my own ears. I allowed my body, poor choices in friends, music, and drugs to speak loudest to me.

Sex, drugs, and alcohol consumed my entire being until the night God called me to be more than some late-night booty call. In Christ, I was finally set free.

Step into my world where I spill my personal tea and break the mug, revealing my brokenness to be made whole again. I'll show you how I made the transition from being fed up to changing up for good!

There will come a point that you will get tired of running around in circles, blaming others for your repeated outcomes. For me, I'll never forget the life changing day that I got fed up! I had a long talk with God and realized I was the one that had to make the change first. We can't control others, but we can control our actions.

I had to be the one to look inside the mirror and say I will never let another man use me again. I am NOT a cheap thrill. I am NOT the one you call last because you failed to get your top pick over to your house. I am somebody's queen and until that special person crosses my path, I'll remain in my palace alone but never lonely because I have the love of God to fill any voids in my life.

I promise you, when you define who you are as a daughter of Christ, you'll learn to value yourself. That's the day you stop being used by others.

Get rid of distractions that make you hot (yup, that one.) You know the ones that look good but deep down you know they're not good for you. When you stand still, stand tall and firm on who you are and what you believe in, life will change dramatically for you too. It won't be easy, but once you truly get tired of being your second best, you will discover a life worth living. Be blessed!

Chapter 1

First Timer

> *"A creature revolting against a creator*
> *is revolting against the source of his own powers*
> *—including even his power to revolt.*
> *It is like the scent of a flower trying to destroy the flower."*
> *~C.S. Lewis*

Turning 18 is like a magic number for a teenage girl. It was the most anticipated year of my life because I was so sheltered and dealt with so many different challenges coming up in the foster system and all. After graduation, I called up my best friend who had turned 18 a bit before me. He was telling me about how it feels to be all grown up. He bragged about the liquor, the chat lines, and his first sexual encounter. Based on his portrayals, I was pumped about turning 18!

Each summer, I visited Ohio leaving Georgia behind. Since I was out of school and could make my own rules, I stayed in Ohio.

I got a job and a car.

I moved in with my best friend, his sister, and her boyfriend. It was their first place. One night after work, we decided to throw a party with just the four of us. My girl, the DJ, put on a R. Kelly CD and we all danced to a slow song drunk and danced in the dark. At some point, Mr. First Timer and I decided to go into the bedroom. I was so intoxicated I fell onto the floor on the way there. He helped me up, asked me if I was okay, picked me up and gently laid me on the bed. He became my official first time. The next morning, he left early, and I woke up to a cold bedside. I had been expecting some cuddle time, a "nice job" or "you want to be my girl?" just like in the movies. But there was nothing. He went about his day as if it were nothing. I was so confused and didn't know what to do next.

Later that day we talked about the 'encounter'. I pleaded with him to be in a relationship with me, but he wanted to be just friends. Our friendship grew more and more awkward because we crossed a line becoming friends with benefits.

Fast forward: He got married and told his wife about our past. She told him he could no longer speak to me at all and just like that, all the years of friendship went down the drain. At first, I was so offended but had to respect her wishes.

Lessons:

Never mix romance with a friendship, it's just not worth possibly losing a friend over. Giving your virginity to a friend does not guarantee you an exclusive relationship. Assumptions can lead to disappointments.

Ladies never go out trying to find a man, instead let him find you.

Don't get so desperate that you will settle for just anybody.

Blessings:

"Watch and pray that ye enter not into temptation: the spirit indeed is willing, but the flesh is weak." ~Matthew 26:41 (KJV)

_____

_____

"No, dear brothers, I am still not all I should be, but I am bringing all my energies to bear on this one thing: Forgetting the past and looking forward to what lies ahead, I strain to reach the end of the race and receive the prize for which God is calling us up to heaven because of what Christ Jesus did for us."

~Philippians 3:13-14 (TLB)

_____

_____

Chapter 2

Green Eyes, Black Lies

*"For where jealousy and selfish ambition exist,
there will be disorder and every vile practice."*
~James 3:16

My coworker and I became really cool at our job. She was my girl! She paid me to take her to a friend's house and I would sit outside in my car waiting for her to finish 'having a good time' with her guy friend. After a few trips, she said her friend's nephew wanted her to introduce him to someone. She explained that I was sitting in the car whenever she was there.

The house was filled with guys, and I wasn't comfortable dropping in for a visit. Eventually, I agreed to meet this guy but refused to go inside. Mr. Green Eyes came out to the car, and we talked. He gave me his phone number and continued to call me for about two weeks straight. He seemed pretty cool, so I agreed to go out with him on a date.

Something was off about him from the beginning. The red flags continued to show once I accepted him as my boyfriend. Toledo is a small town, and everyone knows everyone. In a short amount of time, everybody knew I was dating him. Friends and acquaintances' responses were that they were going to hurt him, and I didn't understand why. With me he was quiet and reserved but I should have paid closer attention to another red flag when my mother didn't like him.

I really enjoyed his company and so did all the other females who were telling me he was so good looking. Shortly after this time together I started receiving phone calls from other women sharing that he was involved with them at the same time he was involved with me. At first, I didn't listen to them and waved it off as jealousy. But when I got a call from my home girl and she confirmed what he was doing, my eyes were opened.

Like a dummy, I continued to 'date' this needy brother that never seemed to have any money for our dates, and always wanted to use my car while I was at work (which I never let him do.)

I decided on Valentine's Day if he did not buy me anything after all the things I'd done for him, then our relationship (I use the word loosely) was over. He showed up with a single rose and an empty card. A week later, I found out that he did not spend the entire holiday with me because he was with another female at a hotel.

Shortly after this disappointment, one night at a friend's house, I recall getting tipsy as a cry for attention. I went for a walk in a drug infested neighborhood certain he would come after me, protect me and show me some love. He did not. (I was blessed to have some good friends that came looking for me and had talked some sense into me.)

He soon drifted off the scene and we didn't speak for the longest time.

Lessons:

His actions defined his true character proving that what everyone was saying about him was true. Pay attention to others' opinions, they are often more correct than looking through 'love-tinted' glasses. After all, everybody cannot be wrong.

Do not give a person too much too soon.

Let a person prove what their lips are saying to you through their actions.

Believe who a person is when they reveal themselves to you.

Blessings:

"Who is wise and understanding among you? Let him show by good conduct that his works are done in the meekness of wisdom." ~James 3:13 (NKJV)

_____

_____

"For the Lord gives wisdom, from His mouth come knowledge and understanding."

~Proverbs 2:6 (NKJV)

_____

_____

"Where there is strife, there is pride, but wisdom is found in those who take advice."

~Proverbs 13:10 (NIV)

_____

_____

Chapter 3
Zodiac Maniac

"Your willingness to look at your darkness
is what empowers you to change."
~Iyanla Vanzant

Time passes and after dealing with two previous fellas, I decided to try something different. I realized I needed a grown man that would provide me with security and would not toy with my emotions. I imagined that older guys wouldn't play with a young girl's heart. I believed they were more mature (more on this) and are not into playing games.

I got on chat lines to have a bit of fun listening to some profiles. It was an 800 number you could call and record a brief description of yourself and what you were looking for in a man. It was like recording a voice mail. Men call up, listen and if they like what they hear, they send you a request to speak further. A lot of the guys were hilarious inside of the party rooms. Back then, those were the DM's and that's where meet ups went down!

One guy beeps in and asked me to connect privately during the chat. So, I did. When we talked, I was actually having a conversation I'd never had before in my life. He taught me the basics of astrology. He educated me on my zodiac sign in such a way that I felt like I was the only Aries on the planet. He dropped knowledge on me and held an intelligent conversation never touching on the topic of sex. I was interested and began to think about longevity with him. We set a time and place to meet.

Whenever I agree to a first date, I take a couple of friends with me to hang out and back me up in case something crazy jumps off. On this date, everything went well. He pulled out a book on astrology, we had a couple of drinks, my friends were in the background giggling along with his friend (he also brought a wingman.) Things went so well I started to see him again and again and often by myself.

As time went on, he often said things to me that should have been red flags but instead I marked them as jokes and nothing too serious. For example, one day he told me that he wanted to marry me and get us a house far out and start a family. Now remind you, I was 18 but I was looking for my soul mate. A friend at work told me to be careful of things like that because it sounded like he wanted to isolate me from friends and family. Another red flag was when he told me that if I ever put my jobs (I had two of them) before him or his sexual desires in the morning that he would burn up my paychecks in front of my face. I foolishly thought that was super funny. I worked hard for my money and who burns up money? I laughed at his 'joke' but his face never changed. He was dead serious.

The more I dated, the more disconnected we became. Looking back, there were so many red flags in this field, you would have sworn the world was in a drought for producing anything of value. Some of his lies included when he told me his baby mama had a key to his house in case of emergencies with their child or when he told me I could no longer spend the night. This list could go on and on. I simply refused to accept what God was showing me about this guy. I only saw what I wanted to see. However, I will say this last event that took place with us was the last straw of my ring of confusion.

I called him up one night and I noticed he sounded a little strange. I asked him what was wrong, and he said, "Nothing." Later that night, he admitted he was in the hospital. I immediately panicked and was concerned because I still cared for him. His 'hospital stay' was actually the birth of a beautiful baby boy that he had just watched enter into this cold world by his baby mama. Yes, you read right. The mother of his other child had just left labor and deliver. When he told me this, my heart dropped, and I thought he was playing a joke on me. He had pulled so many gags on me I thought it was just another one—but this was major. He and I had only been together for a few months, and we all know how long it takes for a full-term baby to prepare for delivery. The math didn't add up. I'd been played.

I did see the baby and we talked outside for a bit. I asked a lot of questions, but I knew anything coming out of his mouth was a lie. I learned he had two kids and strongly suggested he needed to focus on them and his relationship with their mother. Out of there!

Lessons:

Do your research with your eyes wide opened. Know what you're getting into prior to the first date.

Keep God in the center of your choices, and everything will come together.

Do not do all the talking, learn how to listen.

Blessings:

"The mouths of the righteous utter wisdom, and their tongues speak what is just." ~Psalm 37:30 (NIV)

_____

_____

"Be very careful, then, how you live—not as unwise but as wise, making the most of every opportunity, because the days are evil." ~Ephesians 5:15-16 (NIV)

_____

_____

"The fear of the Lord is the beginning of knowledge, but fools despise wisdom and instruction." ~Proverbs 1:7 (NIV)

_____

_____

Chapter 4

Worker's Compensation

"You will be wounded many times in your life. You'll make mistakes.
Some people will call them failures,
but I have learned that failure is really God's way of saying,
'Excuse me, you're going in the wrong direction.'
It's just an experience, just an experience."
~Oprah Winfrey

Let me come right on in with quoting the cliché "Never mix business with pleasure." I had a job where we did a lot of traveling to make sales for this one particular company. Every morning after our meetings we would group up into teams then off we'd go traveling to different cities, making money, and having fun! I can't exactly recall how me, and Mr. Worker's Comp first started talking but after being on the road with each other so often, sharing cool conversations, we decided to pursue one another. We went out for drinks, shared jokes and even discussed our futures with one another. Everything in those moments felt right; so, following our first night of lust and passion, I was hooked on him. I was so smitten I stopped paying attention to the things that mattered to me the most when looking for a boyfriend.

For example, one time he told me that he did not believe in God or Jesus but instead believed in Yahweh. I asked him what that was, and he told me it was a philosophy he was taught in prison. He spelled out his belief in atheism and he continuously tried to get me to follow his values. I chose to just deal with his way of living to save the eventful nights of passion. My goal was to not 'judge him' and respect his way of life if he respected mine.

One night we were driving in my car, and I decided to play some Gospel music. He got so mad because I would not turn off my radio for him and he didn't want to listen to Christian music, that he put my car in park while I was driving at 45 MPH! I drove this maniac to a phone booth (dating myself here) and pretended to call the cops so he would leave.

I'll bet you're wondering if I continued to fool with him, huh? I did. But…that was a major eye opener for me. The last straw was when after he apologized, and I went to go pick him up for work. As I pulled into the apartment complex, he starts walking toward me, but I noticed a female following him with a baseball bat!

She yelled, "Is this the female dog you cheated on me with?" I was shocked and confused and fearful she was going to use that bat on my car. Instead, she went to his car! He grabbed her, ripping her shirt, exposing her breast to everyone in sight. He told me to go to work without him. He picked her up and carried her back inside their apartment. At first, I had no idea who she was but later figured out she was the mother of his children and that was her apartment, not his. I'd fallen for another man who only spoke lies.

Our relationship soon became work gossip. I was in sales, and I went from being the top dealer to a broke dealer. Not only did I learn not to mix business with pleasure, but I also learned not to compromise when it comes to my faith in God.

Lessons:

If someone is an atheist and you are a Christian, it's a recipe for disaster and a tough battle to fight. You need to be with someone who shares your same belief system.

Blessings:

"Don't team up with those who are unbelievers. How can righteousness be partnered with wickedness? How can light live with darkness?" ~2 Corinthians 6:14 (New Living Translation)

_____

_____

"Beyond all these things put on love, which is the perfect bond of unity." ~Colossians 3:14 (NASB)

_____

_____

"Make my joy complete by being of the same mind, maintaining the same love, united in spirit, intent on one purpose." ~Philippians 2:2 (NASB)

_____

_____

"If we say that we have fellowship with Him(Christ) and yet walk in the darkness, we lie and do not practice the truth..." ~1 John 1:6 (NASB)

_____

_____

Chapter 5

The Caring Stripper

> *"My mission in life is not merely to survive,*
> *but to thrive' and to do so with some passion,*
> *some compassion, some humor, and some style."*
> *~ Maya Angelou*

I lost focus on my career and myself, so I felt I needed a fresh start. This is the point where I decided I'd had enough of Ohio and moved back to Georgia. Don't judge me, but at this point, before I left, I let Mr. Green Eyes back into my life. It had been a minute since we had seen or dealt with one another, so when he asked me to take him to Georgian with me so he could turn his life around, I agreed. We were Atlanta bound when he promised me, he would focus on improving our relationship. I was excited and took him up on his offer.

I soon discovered he had written letters to other women telling them he missed them while we were on the trip there! To add insult to injury, he wrote the letters in my special music notebook I kept for my songs.

When we reached Tennessee, my grandmother was driving my car for me because expressways scare me. At the rest stop she saw him looking upset in my car. I told her what had happened and that I wanted him out of my car. As far as I was concerned, he could walk back to Ohio or find another way back. Grandma insisted that it would be wrong of me to leave him wandering on the road miles from home; so, I let him back in the car.

Before we had left Ohio, he told me he needed to go to Chicago to get his birth certificate and he would be gone for a couple of days. Remember that.

Once we arrived in Atlanta, he hooked up with my very resourceful teenage brother. My brother helped him land a good paying job making decent money. One night after he got off work, I heard a car pull up and looked out the window and saw a car slowly driving past my grandmother's house at two o'clock in the morning. I watched Mr. Green Eyes kissing and rubbing all over this female who had given him a ride. I silently screamed and bawled my eyes out.

You'd think I'd learn, but worse yet, I answered the phone one night to a 17-year-old girl calling from Ohio, asking for him. She thought I was his cousin, so we talked openly. She told me he had plans for moving her down south with him after she graduated from high school. The sick thing was he was in his twenties, and she was a minor and they'd been hooked up for some time. I was furious! In fact, that's an understatement! She thought he was staying with family to stay out of trouble. When I told her the truth, she was more upset than I was.

Remember when I said take note of when he went to Chicago for his birth certificate? Truthfully, he went there to make love to his honey one last time before heading south. She was in a gang, and he really shouldn't have messed with her feelings. He told her he left for Georgia because someone in Ohio was trying to set him up. When she called me, she told me she had a relative that worked for the FBI. Apparently, she had thoroughly investigated my house and our things. I mean she was even able to tell me how many steps I had INSIDE MY HOUSE! She knew the color of my house and details she shouldn't have had. She planned on getting revenge on my family because he fed her lies about being held hostage from our family in Ohio. She believed him and was ready to fend her love for him.

He came in from work that night while I was still on the phone with Chicago, and I told him someone wanted to talk to him. I handed him the phone. He looked so surprised you would have thought he saw a ghost! He couldn't face me and could hardly swallow.

I didn't want him in the house or the same city. I wanted him out immediately! It was late and I didn't want to wake my grandparents to ask for directions to the bus station, so while we waited for morning, I took a knife to all his clothes and poured red dye inside all of his white shoes. The hate was real! I was ready to pay for a bus ticket back to Ohio. I knew he would say he didn't have the money and I was sick and tired of his excuses. I asked my grandmother for directions to the bus station, and she told me I was wrong and should let him stay. She told me it was not "Christian-like" to do to him like he had done to me. I argued that I didn't want him in the house, and she responded that it was her house, and she would decide who stayed. She was willing to let him stay until his new girlfriend took him in.

I was so hurt and down that I was cried out. I talked to all my girls to ease the pain, but I could still feel it. So, one night I saw this club and decided to drive by it. I stopped and talked to a couple of gentlemen at the door. I found out they were male dancers and they invited me to their show. When I went inside, it seemed as if my wildest dreams had come true! Everything I had ever wanted physically in a man was right there on stage.

After a couple of months of going to the strip club every week, I wanted to give this one particular dancer a try. He looked good, smelled great and treated me right. The thought never crossed my mind that he worked for tips and thus his treatment of me. Oh! The drinks and the eye candy! When he would talk to me, he expressed real concern and gave me sound advice on some things. I was so sucked into the club scene that it became like an underground world for me. I had to have my nails done with the black tip and the silver lining, the pedicure to match, flawless hair, and the seductive outfits to match every week. That way when I went on stage to tip him, the women would feel me, but the dancer would enjoy my physical eye candy as well.

Now listen, if you are dating a stripper, there are certain codes to follow. Ridiculous as it may sound, you must realize that you will never be "the only woman" because they are going to pull whatever tricks out of their bags to get top dollar along with fulfilling their sexual desires. The more they are willing to do at a private party and even on stage, the more money they get paid. It's as simple as that. Even though this guy was pretty cool, I spent a lot of nights alone and had to wait for him to finish whatever or whoever he was doing before he would get with me. I became his sloppy seconds.

Lessons:

Don't be fooled by "all that glitters is gold". Value yourself enough to stay away from players.

Blessings:

"Charm is deceitful, and beauty is vain, but a woman who fears the Lord is to be praised."

~Proverbs 31:30 (NASB)

_____

_____

"I will praise You, for I am fearfully and wonderfully made; Marvelous are Your works; and that my soul knows very well." ~Psalms 139:14 (NKJV)

_____

_____

"Your beauty should not come from outward adornment, such as elaborate hairstyles and the wearing of gold jewelry or fine clothes. Rather, it should be that of your inner self, the unfading beauty of a gentle and quiet spirit, which is of great worth in God's sight."

~1 Peter 3:3-4 (NIV)

_____

_____

Chapter 6

The Heartless Stripper

"If you are silent about your pain,
they'll kill you and say you enjoyed it."
~Zora Neale Hurston

What one man did not fulfill; I would find another man that would. Now my thoughts were, if they can do it, so can I. I fell right into their little traps and never even realized it. The joke was all on me though as I became their private conversations on who had me first and who could sleep with the girl in black. Now just when I thought I had seen it all, arriving on the scene was a seven-foot chocolate wonder! He owned the stage, and he brought a sense of comedy to the floor as he performed. Every woman in there wanted just one night with him. Yes, one night was all I needed.

I had become a regular at the club. I met this female in there and we instantly became friends. She would sleep with one stripper, and I'd sleep with another stripper. We would laugh and joke and discuss our sexual experiences and these dudes. One day, I guess she got tired of me mentioning Mr. Heartless name, so she told me one day, "Fool, he don't love you!" I argued her down about how close the two of us were getting and that we were becoming more than just sex partners. Around this time, I was close to my 19th birthday, but she was already in her 30's and she turned me on to how the game works with men. She told me to tell him I was pregnant, and I said, "But we use protection." She said for me to tell him the condom must have broken and to see what he says. I mustered up enough guts to tell him exactly what she told me, and he nicely asked me to get rid of the baby. He had already conceived 12 other children (I kid you not!) by other women and he didn't want any more.

He failed the test suggested by my friend that proved it was nothing more than a fling. He didn't even offer to pay for the abortion. He told me to ask someone else for the money. He told me to call him after I had terminated the pregnancy. He coached me to just go, lay down and take it easy afterwards. It made me wonder how many other females he had said that to. It made me realize what it would be like if I really had been pregnant.

This was just another cheap thrill at my own expense. It was all about my body for his pleasure, my tipping to pay his bills as well as child support and my loyalty to him. Tough lesson, but my friend was right.

Lessons:

You are a child of the King, a princess. Understanding who you are designed to be is the first step to moving away from things that are designed to demean your true identity and moving toward the incredible person God intended you to be.

Always learn from your mistakes so you won't repeat them. Never lie to a man and say that you are pregnant just to get him to stay. You'll have to tell one lie after the other to keep up with the trimesters and beyond that, it could get really messy. Even life threatening.

Blessings:

"And blessed is she who believed that the Lord would fulfill His promises to her." ~Luke 1:45 (NIV)

_____

_____

"She is clothed with strength and dignity; she can laugh at the days to come." ~Proverbs 31:25 (NIV)

_____

_____

"She is more precious than rubies, nothing you desire can compare with her." ~Proverbs 3:15 (NIV)

_____

_____

"God is within her; she shall not fall; God will help her at break of day." ~Psalm 46:5 (NIV)

_____

_____

Chapter 7

B-List Celebrity

"Deal with yourself as an individual worth of respect,
and make everyone else deal with you the same way."
~Nikki Giovanni

Moving right along, here comes a guy well known locally and he is always hosting events for household name celebrities. This man was a comedian both on and off stage. When I was around Mr. Celebrity, I felt like I had it all. He kept it real with me on most things. He told me about other well-known people that I needed to stay away from. He told me who I should gravitate toward, and he shared with me just how our friendship could benefit each other.

One day at his house, we shared drinks, a good movie and a good laugh! As I arrived, I sipped on a glass of bubbly and plopped down beside him. His smoldering eyes held mine and he said he wanted to take me on a trip out of town. We were going first class, limousine, hotel and all expenses paid. What a step up from my previous relationships!

He explained there would be two other comedians in the limo with us (whose names I will not disclose either) and I would not be allowed to speak to them at all. It was a pimp thing. He did say that the other gentlemen would have a lady with them as well and we all had to keep quiet.

"What? REALLY?" I screamed. "When did I become your whore, cause I missed that memo."

So now I was a trophy? I quickly dropped him like a bad habit along with the trip offer.

I directly let him know that I was not a groupie and how dare he ask me to be involved in this situation. He apologized and begged me for my forgiveness. He even sent me a few text messages to see if I could attend a few of his upcoming events but I still declined. Celebrity or not, I just decided this was not the kind of life for me. I hear his name on the radio and we have bumped into each other a few times because we are both performers, but I've stood my ground. It is awkward though because when we do bump into each other he, just stares at me for long periods of time.

After this incident, I chose to cool my heels for a bit, and chill with just my girls. I still needed to look deep inside myself to figure out why these things kept happening to me. I needed to face facts. I thought hanging out with the ladies would help me to gain insight. I did discover that running caused even more issues.

Lessons:

Running just brings current issues to new locations and makes things worse.

Begin today to value yourself.

Blessings:

"For You created my inmost being; you knit me together in my mother's womb." ~Psalm 139:13 (NIV)

_____

_____

"Being confident of this very thing, that He who began a good work in you will perform it until the day of Jesus Christ." ~Philippians 1:6 (KJV)

_____

_____

"You are altogether beautiful, my love; there is no flaw in you." ~Song of Solomon 4:7 (ESV)

_____

_____

Chapter 8

Jamaican Rapist

"Take chances, make mistakes. That's how you grow.
Pain nourishes your courage.
You have to fail in order to practice being brave."
~ Mary Tyler Moore

One night, me and my girls decided to hang out and shake off whatever was bothering us all. I got my crew together and we rolled out in my car. That night, we decided to hang out downtown Atlanta. There was a major car show going on and as a teenager born in the small city of Toledo, Ohio, this seemed very fun and adventurous! There were people there by the truckloads showing off their vehicles. One truck in particular was an all-blue pickup monster on wheels that had a custom-made Choo Choo train horn installed! The whole downtown area was loud and popping that night!

Cruising down the street, we stopped at a red light right next to this white car. This car had two handsome fellas in it, and they were really concerned with the contents of my car's interior–ladies! We ignored them and giggled for a while as we stopped at the different lights before giving in and rolling down the window.

The driver was light skinned with a confident smile and black shades that screamed for attention. The passenger was dark skinned with the long brown dreads of a Goddess. At first, the driver was into my friend on the passenger's side but after we all started talking to one another, he gave his number to me.

A month or two later, me and this gentleman hooked up at a Jamaican restaurant in Decatur and over dinner we officially gave the relationship department a try. He introduced me to some of his family and I thought that was a major forward move. I heard that if a man introduces you to his family that means he genuinely has an interest in you. Otherwise, he would have kept you his little secret. I discovered, that may be true in some cases, but it was not true in mine. I mean he really had me thinking that I could finally settle down. He even told me that he had a daughter that his mom had custody of. He also told me he lost custody because he did not know how to raise up a girl. I volunteered that if we were going to be together that I could pitch in. To this day I am a firm believer in children living with their parents and giving the grandparents the freedom to enjoy their golden years. He asked me to go downtown with him to meet his main cousin at his work.

As we entered the store to meet his cousin, Mr. Jamaican introduces us. His cousin asked me if I had any sisters or friends as beautiful as me. Now one of my sisters was already married but the other two were babies so I didn't mention them. I did tell him about my friend/coworker. People at work that knew her longer than me told me she was pretty loose with the guys. I didn't want to judge her, and she seemed cool at least with me. We never really hung out outside of work, but I did take her home on a few occasions. I'll just call her Dee to protect her privacy. Dee was the one I decided to introduce my boyfriend's cousin to. Mr. Jamaican asked us to come over after work one morning and we did. We got off at 7am and as soon as we clocked out, we were on our way to his spot to have a good time!

When we arrived , Mr. Jamaican had eggs and bacon already made for me with a glass of peach juice. I thought his kindness was romantic. He told me to go ahead and eat breakfast while he ran to pick up his cousin from the train station. I started drinking the juice to wash my food down and noticed it tasted funny. I had my friend try it too and she confirmed it tasted funny. I didn't finish the whole glass, but I did have a good portion. I assumed it was some Jamaican drink or something. No big deal. I put the glass down and enjoyed the morning. When the guys got back from the station, we were all in the living room on the couch talking. They had two black cans of cheap beer (and we all know cheap beer gets you messed up) that we started sipping. Shortly after, we moved to the backyard and started smoking some weed. My boyfriend and I decided to head up to the bedroom to get a bit more comfortable and private.

I remember him pulling my pants down so we could have sex. It was protected sex, but it seemed very short and then I blacked out. Next thing I knew, I slowly opened my eyes to find his cousin naked on top of me and inside me with no condom on. He kept asking me if I knew who was "sexing" me. I was naked too and didn't even have my glasses on. I was slowly gaining awareness of the fact that something was wrong, and I had been drugged. When I realized who he was I pushed him off me and yelled "NO!"

I was shocked and in disbelief and a million thoughts racing through my head: "Where's my friend? Do I have AIDS? How did this happen?" Since I was unclothed, I grabbed the blanket off the bed and quickly wrapped it around me so I could go find my friend and boyfriend. Struggling into the next room down the hall, Dee was laying on the bed and Mr. Jamaican, fully clothed was sitting in a chair next to her and they were talking.

They didn't appear to have had sex, but I wasn't sure how long I'd been out, and anything could have happened. He met me in the bathroom so we could talk. When I told him what happened he seemed very unbothered by it all. He did try to fake being angry, but it was easy to spot it wasn't genuine at all. He then told me to take a shower, try to relax and he was going to confront his cousin.

Mr. Jamaican created a melodramatic scene when he approached his cousin. It seemed so staged. Long story short, he muscled the guy into the car and told me and Dee he'd be back after dropping him off at the train station. When they left, I told my friend what happened, and I passed out again. When I woke up this time, I was in another room and Dee was with me looking out for me to be sure I was okay.

When Mr. Jamaican returned, he told me not to say anything to anyone and especially not to his brother who owned the house. I finally was able to get myself together and we were out of there by noon.

On the way home, we stopped at a grocery store, but the rest of the drive was eerie and quiet, as if someone had died. We drove slowly as we put the pieces together. She calmly said, "Teaira, you were set up." I cried not believing someone could be so cruel.

Over the next few days, I remained in my room wearing sweatpants on my couch. I called my job and told them I was dealing with a crisis and could not make it to work. Finally on day three, my mother called and asked me what was wrong. I hesitated to tell her what went down but a mother knows when something is wrong with her child. When I got the story out, she was furious! She insisted I get the proper authorities involved. I told her I had made a deal with both guys that if they agreed to take an AIDS test with me and it came back negative that I would just move on. My mom was still not having it and convinced me to seek help from the hospital and the police.

The day for us to meet up at the AIDS center for testing arrived. The men who took my blood sample were very angry when they found out the rapist and his accomplice were both in the waiting area waiting to get their results as well. It took everything in my healthcare professionals' power not to beat these guys down in the lobby. He escorted me out to my car after the negative results were in and he comforted me along the way.

When they gave me the rape kit, they gave me a morning after pill. They shined a bright light over my body to see if there were any traces of DNA still present on my body. The DA got involved instantly. The police picked me up and took me to their downtown office as well. Although every test was negative, I did contract HPV, so they had to monitor me over the next two years. They said my blood cells appeared cancerous after they performed a colposcopy on me. A colposcopy is a method of examining the cervix, vagina, and vulva with a surgical instrument and is a screening test used to identify abnormal cervical cells.

I literally thought my life was over. I was the youngest person on the floor where they would test and treat cancer patients. I often received stares from my elders. I guess they were trying to figure out why I was up there with them. The procedures were painful as they clipped samples of my insides for further testing.

The "cousin" was eventually caught by the police after hiding out. He faced time for my rape charge, resisting arrest and child endangerment charges. They did not arrest my ex because they said by law, he physically did nothing wrong. As for the guy that raped me, the DA told me he would be the one to decide if we should go to trial or not. He also said if we did go to trial, the jury would take under consideration that I was intoxicated and may have agreed to consensual sex. If you are confused about what I was told that makes two of us.

Here's another thing. Come to find out, that wasn't even Jamaica's biological cousin either. They were just friends and the name that he gave me was just a nick name for his cousin.

Dee played ignorant to the DA and the detective because she did not want to get involve. I'm not sure what they said to her, but she seemed scared to speak up. It made me wonder if she could have been in on the rape as well. I should have left her alone just like my coworkers told me to do in the first place.

I eventually quit my job because it was difficult facing everyone treating me like one big charity case thanks to Dee spilling all the details. The gossiping was unbearable. It struck me odd that she knew all the details for the office gossip but knew nothing when the detectives asked for her side of things.

I am proud to announce that out of all this drama, the doctor can no longer find traces of HPV. All of my pap smears are normal. It took a few years to gain clearance, but God is indeed good! All the time!

Lessons:

I would not wish rape on my worst enemy but if something like this happens to you or a loved one, whatever you do, DO NOT SHOWER until you have gone to the hospital and received a rape kit. I know you may feel disgusted at the time but showering washes away the evidence needed to prove your case. I believe he knew this already.

Blessings:

"For God did not send His Son into the world to condemn the world, but that the world through Him might be saved." ~ John 3:17 (KJV)

_____

_____

"Never take your own revenge, beloved, but leave room for the wrath of God, for it is written: 'Vengeance is mine, I will repay,' says the Lord." ~Romans 12:19 (NASB)

_____

_____

"Beloved, do not be surprised at the fiery ordeal among you, which comes upon you for the testing, as though something strange were happening to you; but to the degree that you share the sufferings of Christ, keep on rejoicing, so that at the revelation of His glory you may also rejoice and be overjoyed."

~ 1 Peter 4:12-13

_____

_____

Chapter 9
Drug Thug

"Trust yourself.
Create the kind of self that you'll be happy to live with all your life.
Make the most of yourself by fanning the tiny,
inner sparks of possibility into flames of achievement. "
~ Golda Meir

Here I go again, out on the scene giving love another try. I visited a park in Stone Mountain for a family reunion. Me and my friend left the group and headed up the mountain by ourselves to check out the scenery from up high! I was looking for a lighter to light up my cigar, but I must have dropped it. There was a young man up there who was smoking so we joined him. I asked for a light, and he did just that. He even shared with us what he was smoking. Before we left, we shared numbers.

One day I called him, and we had a great time together. We went to the drive in to watch movies, we would drink, smoke, and have our own little private parties. Sometimes he would have me cracking up because he never wanted to sit in one spot for too long without being irritated. I learned this was due to the lifestyle he was living. He would be so paranoid we couldn't stay in one place for very long.

One day I got a call from the mother of his children (here we go again!) The first time she called I was everything kind of name but a child of God to her. I never have been one to argue over a man, especially if he is not my husband. So, the next time we talked, I set a tranquil tone. She also decided to be more peaceable and talk it out like two adults. We realized it was him that was playing the both of us. She told me he had children with her as well as someone else. She also told me she got my number out of his phone while he was asleep. She offered to meet up with me to introduce me to her son, but it was just not worth my time, gas or trouble. I never could understand why a person would not mention their children. I understand not bringing your seed around your dates and flings but when you are talking about moving in with one another, getting a house together, and being committed at what point do you mention that you have a child? Later he did mention he had a son.

Now I must admit there were certain signs with him that I should have paid more attention to. For example, we were supposed to be moving in together but when it was time to view the property and fill out the paperwork, something would always come up on his end. That should have told me that he had something to hide. He had warrants. I ignored it. But the baby momma incident was the last straw.

Lessons:

God always shows you signs but you must be willing to look out for them and accept what it is that's being revealed to you without second guessing all the time.

God Values you.

Blessings:

"For I know the plans I have for you, says the Lord, plans for peace and not for evil, to give you a future and a hope." ~Jeremiah 29:11 (NASB)

_____

_____

"Therefore I, the prisoner of the Lord, urge you to walk in a manner worthy of the calling with which you have been called, with all humility and gentleness, with patience, bearing with on another in love..." ~Ephesians 4:1-2 (NASB)

_____

_____

"A wise person is cautious and turns away from evil, but a fool is arrogant and careless."

~Proverbs 14:16 (NASB)

_____

_____

Chapter 10

Fed Up

*"I believe that telling our stories, first to ourselves
and then to one another and the world, is a revolutionary act.
It is an act that can be met with hostility, exclusion, and violence.
It can also lead to love, understanding, transcendence, and
community."*
~ Janet Mock

Here I am at age 19 getting ready to turn 20 now just reflecting over my life. I had a one-on-one with myself and realized that something had to change, and that change had to start with me. At this moment, I felt as if I had created all this unnecessary drama on my own. I viewed every single black man both young and old as low down. I felt that had I been a little more respectful to my temple, a lot of this could have been avoided. At this moment in my life, I remember feeling that I am worth more than good looks, nice curves, and a free sexual ride. I am respect, I am loved, and I have a purpose. I am a good woman who deserves a good man. I had to stop playing house to people that were just playing me. Most importantly, it was time that I took responsibility for my own actions and went back to my roots of self-worth.

For the first time in a long time, I prayed to God and told Him that I was tired of being a late night snack for vultures. I wanted a husband. I told Him that I did not want to wake up to a cold body beside me anymore. I wanted an actual companionship and love. I mean, I really cried out to God himself on that day! It was as if my heart did all the talking because I completely gave God everything that I had within me that night that screamed out help! As I cried, I felt comforted because God's hand of mercy was all over my life. Brace yourself for what happened next because this was the greatest surprise of my life, and I did not see this happening so soon. But, when you seek God with your whole heart, it's an amazing feeling! You just feel set free and so clean! This is when He reveals himself!

Lesson:

If you seek God first with your whole heart and stop trying to 'fix' things yourself, he will give you the very things you want the most. God knows your address; he'll send a life partner to your front porch. Trust Him.

Blessings:

"Be still and know that I am God; I will be exalted among the nations, I will be exalted in the earth." ~Psalm 46:10 (NIV)

_____

_____

"His unchanging plan has always been to adopt us into his own family by sending Jesus Christ to die for us. And he did this because he wanted to! Now all praise to God for his wonderful kindness to us and his favor that he has poured out upon us because we belong to his dearly loved Son."

~Ephesians 1:5-6 (TLB)

_____

_____

"Others died that you might live; I traded their lives for yours because you are precious to me and honored, and I love you." ~Isaiah 43:4 (TLB)

_____

_____

Chapter 11

The Search

"Stories are memory aids,
instruction manuals and moral compasses."
~ Aleks Krotoski

One day at my grandmother's house, my annoying little brother was coming at me. I was already angry that day for some reason, so I thought that he came into my bedroom to be even more irritating.

My brother called to me so many times that I finally snarled, "What?" He replies back, "I have a friend that wants to meet you."

So, I quickly opened the door with the biggest attitude ever and on the other side I see this 6-foot monster standing on the sidewalk waiting for me to greet him. I looked at him and I said, "yes" as in ok what do you want? He had a confident smile on his face, and he could not seem to get the words out fast enough. I slammed the door right in his face and ran upstairs right back into my room while yelling at my little mini me.

I asked my brother why he invited this dude to the house. He got a little buff with me and said, "Well, you said you wanted a good man and somebody that had some business about himself, so I thought I'd help you out sis."

Come to find out his name was Greg and boy did I quickly learn who this man was because this gentleman was consistently coming by to try and pursue me. Every time I turned around; there he was. Eventually, when Greg would come over, we would all just start chilling with one another inside the car. The more we began to communicate, the more I began to open up to him. He was so easy to talk to and he was a good listener which was a bonus for me! When we would engage in conversation, this brother could talk about anything for hours and it was not always about sex and the chemistry just started forming on its own.

When talking together, I discovered we had a lot in common. We were both raised by our grandparents, we both respected our elders, we had no baby momma/daddy drama, and the list went on. It all just seemed too perfect though. So perfect that I would try and tarnish the flame between us every chance I got.

It's strange that I had been mistreated for so long that I didn't know how to embrace the goodness in a new person. (Please don't let that be you.) I needed to open my eyes and be prepared to receive what I had been praying to God for. At first, I was constantly looking for a reason to leave, I even tried to make him leave me. If I made a mistake, I thought it was over. Sounds crazy, doesn't it? But when you have been mistreated for so long, it's easy to feel like the right thing is the wrong thing.

I was going on 20, so all the adults, family, friends and even my enemies had something to say about our relationship. I learned not to let everyone all up in my business. Too much '2 cents' causes non-sense.

Following the puppy love stage, Greg went back to his home state for a while to clear his head. He and his family had a huge falling out leaving him with no place to go. That was around the same time that we called off our relationship because some of his family did not want us together. I did not want to stand in the way of his family, so I agreed to back away from the relationship although Greg felt we should still be together. I grew up in foster care, so I felt like family was everything, even if they were wrong. I did not want to be the cause of a family breaking up.

For months and months, I had been asking around for Greg once I knew he'd moved. No one seemed to know where he was including his family. At one point no one could locate any of them. A few months later, I got a call and because the voice was so distinctive, I knew who it was. I was super excited to hear him! By now I had just moved into my first apartment. It was a hole in the wall, but it was mine. Since it was in the hood, I asked him if he could stay the night with me for at least one week so that I could get used to living on my own.

Without hesitation he came to stay with me. That week turned into a decade of love and still counting! I cannot end this chapter without saying that he is my King, my stabilizer, and my rock! Being with him taught me that not all black men are the same and that there are still some good men out there.

He is the father of all my children, my lover, and my fighter. I'll love him forever and a day for everything he has ever been to me. In fact, I told him about the HPV and that it could be cancerous and asked if he would still want to be with me. He said he would love me no matter what. The doctor cleared me on this issue.

Lesson:

I am a living witness that no matter what the situation may be whenever you truly get fed up, you have to change up or you'll continue to be in the same loop, repeating the same drama with different faces. In my story, the change had to begin with me. I'm just grateful that during my transitional period, God placed the answer to my prayers right into my path.

Blessings:

"And the Lord will guide you continually, and satisfy you with all good things, and keep you healthy too; and you will be like a well-watered garden, like an ever-flowing spring."

~Isaiah 58:11 (TLB)

_____

_____

"Remember, too, that knowing what is right to do and then not doing it is sin." ~James 4:17 (TLB)

_____

_____

Chapter 12 (Part II)

The Beginning (Meant to Be)

*"I had to make my own living and my own opportunity.
But I made it!
Don't sit down and wait for opportunities to come.
Get up and make them."*
~Madam C.J. Walker

Teaira's Story:

At this point, I was the biggest party animal, and I did whatever I felt like I needed to do to ease the pain from the assault. I did two things well: I worked hard, and I played harder. After my first job ended, I found myself needing to do something with my time, so I would head over to my boyfriend's house who was still living with his mom and stepdad. We were playing dominos and smoking on goodies when Greg's father-in-law kept interrupting our game. After several interruptions of, "Greg come here," I could feel the negative energy building. I asked Greg what was wrong. He said, "My stepdad is upset that you won't take me to the laundry mat." I was shocked that after working two jobs that he didn't understand that I needed to just chill.

I was done. Greg's father-in-law had cussed him out for the last time. I drove my boyfriend to his sister's house and broke up with him. Being a product of the foster system, the last thing I wanted to do was cause division in his family like I had experienced. Soon after, Greg left town for a few months. I had no idea where he relocated. I asked the block a few times, but he was told he was gone for good.

I returned to being myself until I met a new friend. He had a way about himself and when I discovered he was a drug dealer, I had to give it a taste. This is the guy I mentioned earlier. Stay with me.

Greg's Story:

After a heated argument in the house, my girlfriend, took me to my sister's house. Before she drove off, she said, "I think it's best if we break up." Here I thought the night couldn't get any worse. I listened to her reasoning and reluctantly I accepted. What else could I do at this point? I just agreed and tried to gather my thoughts.

My sister and her boyfriend calmed me down and told me I could stay and get myself together. I thanked them and within that same week, I was on my way back to Minnesota. When I first stepped off the bus, I could feel all the feelings of love, joy and even the pain that I previously tried to run away from. I felt the love of my family here and the pain of losses here as well. I made my way around the city traveling old roads to see what had changed and a lot had changed. I paid a visit to my uncle's house, and they let me stay with them. My thoughts after seeing everybody was that now it's time to get some money the fastest way possible.

The streets were easy to get back into but there was something different about it this time. I tried to smoke and drink the feeling away, but it was still there. Something was telling me to stop. Then one day I was thinking about my grandmother, and I was so high I started seeing everything differently. I couldn't move or do anything. I could only sit still and watch what was going on all around me. For the first time I was seeing things for what they really were.

I tried to tell someone what had happened, but they all just laughed and said you are high. Shortly after that, things got worse, and a war broke out in the streets. Money stopped. Hanging out stopped. And the truth started revealing itself. I was living in fear but didn't know what it was. Then I got an offer to go back to Georgia. When I looked at my current situation, I took the offer.

Now back in Atlanta, I felt peace. I got a job, and everything seemed like it was going good but I knew it would only last so long. As I planned my next steps, I started smoking again. My mom came into my room and said, "Here's some clothes I found when you left." I put them in my closet and one of my pants had money in them. I checked the other pockets and found five dollars, a bag of weed and a phone number. I looked at the number and was surprised. For the next two days I couldn't stop thinking about her. I decided to see what might become of calling her. I dialed the number and to my shock, Teaira answered the phone!

I was cool on the phone but on the inside, I was doing backflips!

Teaira:

I'm at my grandmother's house and my cell phone rings with "Mike Jones" as my ringtone (don't judge me.) I answered it, "Hello? Who is this? Wow! Greg how are you doing?" With my hand on my chest, I gasped for air. I was so surprised and shocked that he still remembered my number. It didn't take long for us to get reacquainted and hanging out again. I remember the moment we made love for the first time in the car, God was not present, but we vowed to always love each other.

I even reminisced on the time my cheating ex "Green Eyes" thought that I had robbed his bank account and things got really ugly over the phone between us, so I went to his job to check him. I told Greg to stay in the car, but he wasn't having it and followed me in. Greg was down for whatever may have happened between me and Green Eyes. The security Greg gave me and the countless ways he had been there for me really turned me on. The flashbacks were coming and going faster than a fixed income and we had so many similarities. For example, both of our grandmothers raised us, both of our grannies had the same middle names, and we both were misunderstood by our family. He had a way of intently listening to me whenever I spoke and that really excited me.

Memories quickly vanished once I got back inside the house because my grandmother and I had gotten into it once again. My ex kept coming by even after cheating on me several times, but my grandmother still welcomed him at the house because he didn't know many people in Atlanta. What!!??

I reached a breaking point and moved out. My friend, Felicia, 12 years older than me, advised me to go down into the country with her so that I could get some male clients to strip for. She shouted, "Tee that's where the real money is!" I thought about it but I realized I was not about that life, so I backed out. Her other suggestion was to start buying household items for my new place to visualize my own home, so that's the advice I chose.

I moved to the hood. This was the first time being in my own spot and it was scary. I asked Greg to come stay with me for a week or so until I got used to the new place. The same week I moved in was also the same week my job was shut down. I told Greg what had happened, and he said, "I'll donate my whole check to whatever you need." Instantly, we shared everything. We moved in with the intentions of being roommates, but that was far too much temptation. Old flames decided to call me back but by then it was too late. I wanted Greg and Greg only! We got an AIDS test, and we took everything to the next level. Old friends, nagging family and the single life started disappearing very quickly. For an example, we went over to Felicia's house to babysit her newborn baby so that she could enjoy a night out after having the little guy. She came to the door wearing her T-shirt and panties. I learned that she was jealous of Greg, so she had to go. Felicia had to lay on her back with random men for everything she had; I didn't have to do that.

After that hump, I soon started working at the airport and we combined our money. We had a ton of parties with our friends and if they were not there the party still went on. We both became heavy drinkers and pornography would help to get our private parties started. Party going, porn watching, then sex making was the cycle in our house. One thing though, this apartment was strange. For instance, we had gotten into a huge argument one night and the pictures of our grandmothers fell on the floor. Things moved by themselves, rats, roaches, and squirrels invaded our privacy. The slumlord was jailed due to excessive codes violations. It was indeed time to bounce. We threw away old pictures of past relationships and we decluttered our space. We packed light and moved to a much nicer apartment.

Lessons:

The devil will use any means to win you to him. When you invite evil to surround you, you give Satan more territory in your life. Listen to the red flags and shut evil down the moment you see it.

Blessings:

"You made all the delicate, inner parts of my body and knit them together in my mother's womb. Thank you for making me so wonderfully complex! It is amazing to think about. Your workmanship is marvelous—and how well I know it. You were there while I was being formed in utter seclusion!"

~Psalm 139:13-15 (TLB)

_____

_____

"So, here's what I want you to do, God helping you: Take your everyday, ordinary life—your sleeping, eating, going-to-work, and walking-around life—and place it before God as an offering. Embracing what God does for you is the best thing you can do for him. Don't become so well-adjusted to your culture that you fit into it without even thinking. Instead, fix your attention on God. You'll be changed from the inside out. Readily recognize what he wants from you, and quickly respond to it. Unlike the culture around you, always dragging you down to its level of immaturity, God brings the best out of you, develops well-formed maturity in you." ~Romans 12: 1 (the Message)

_____

_____

Chapter 13

Setting the Foundation

"You can't just sit there and wait for people to give you that golden dream. You've got to get out there and make it happen for yourself."
~Diana Ross

Things started looking up. Greg sent out a video recording of me trying out for Tyler Perry's new show that was coming out. I sang, "Step Aside" off of his "Daddy's Little Girl" soundtrack and I received a call back a year later to become a featured extra. I missed the initial call and withing five minutes of returning the call, that spot was filled. Greg held down two jobs so that I could start going to college and chasing my dreams of becoming a famous singer. I worked part time at the airport, and I'd come home from break just to make sweet love to my man! When I would go back to work, my nosy co-workers could tell that I was getting it in on break.

I started my own singing business and would negotiate my own deals as a background vocalist. I put together my very first concert and people knew me as Lady Tee.

"Lady Tee. Was that you singing at Holyfield's house?"

"Yes, that was me," I put out an ad for another background vocalist to join forces with me that's how I met Crystal. She was so different from any other females that I knew because she was my age, married, extremely devoted to church, and could sing her heart out! Greg and I did not attend Pastor Dollar's church for the longest time because we heard rumors about his ministry. For example, 'they' said you had to submit your tax forms to sit on the first few rows, the ATM is in the lobby area by the doors, and it was said that Pastor only taught on prosperity. We went anyway to visit his church one day, and it changed our lives!

Come to find out, paying taxes to sit up front was a lie. We sat up front so close to his wife we could have tapped her on the shoulder. We never witnessed an ATM in the lobby but if we had, that's a brilliant idea being that most people carry plastic instead of paper. We watch his mission trips overseas and what he does for the community on a daily basis. It was evident people who made up these lies had never been to his church before. We eventually joined this church, and we were blessed tremendously. We began premarital classes and were later married there.

We returned to partying, and we didn't have a care in the world. Money was constantly flowing into our bank accounts until one day we looked up and could not pay our bills. We put all our monies into one bank account and used our one and only debit card to buy business cards online. A third-party "phished" and got a hold of our information. They stole from us for a few months before we caught on. My bank told us we were a part of a major scam operating out of Canada, so I called the 800 numbers of the scammer they posed as different companies with the same greeting but different names. The bank did not give us any of that money back and their response was to pay close attention next time to the fine print when shopping online.

Moments later, I received a call from Greg, "Baby have you been in the house today?"

"No," I said, "I'm at school."

"We've been robbed." Someone had the nerve to steal Greg's $300 video game, cigarettes, and a box of condoms! We put all of that down on the police report (yes, the condoms too!) As strange as it may seem these situations brought us closer together because we knew we had each other's backs no matter what.

In the middle of all of this chaos my boyfriend asked, "Will you marry me?"

My answer was yes, but I wanted to do this the old-fashioned way. I called my father who lived a few states away and asked him for his blessings. To my surprise, my father obliged. We rented a car and traveled to Ohio only to be letdown. Dad had said his girlfriend of twenty plus years was tripping so to keep peace he was not able to see us. I cried and cussed the whole trip back home. Finally, we arrived in Atlanta and decided we would go through our contact list and gather up some bridesmaids and grooms-men. We heard: "I'm too busy." "I would but the wedding attire cost too much." "I don't know about this, y'all are getting married way too soon." These were the excuses we were told. I remember wondering why everyone was bailing out on me. I struggled with feeling like a nobody, and that no one wanted to support us. Greg had always been told by his mother that Greg didn't actually exist so that was a dead end too. We decided to just go to our premarital classes and marry despite all this.

The identity theft wiped us out and required us to move. No address to transfer to, no one to say "Yes, y'all can move in with us," and nowhere to go. We found ourselves homeless and without a wedding.

Lessons:

When you are truly in love with someone, there is no need to have an entourage. When it comes down to the wedding, all you need is a party of two. The bride and groom are the most important components for your big day.

Blessings:

"Don't be obsessed with getting more material things. Be relaxed with what you have. Since God assured us, "I'll never let you down, never walk off and leave you," we can boldly quote, God is there, ready to help; I'm fearless no matter what. Who or what can get to me?" ~Hebrews 13:5 (The Message)

_____

_____

"It is better to be poor and honest than rich and cheater." ~Proverbs 28:6 (TLB)

_____

_____

"What's the price of a pet canary? Some loose change, right? And God cares what happens to it even more than you do. He pays even greater attention to you, down to the last detail—even numbering the hairs on your head! So don't be intimidated by all this bully talk. You're worth more than a million canaries." ~ Matthew 10: 29-31 (the Message)

_____

_____

Chapter 14

Through it all, "I do"

"Courage means to keep making forward progress
while you still feel afraid."
~Joyce Meyers

Talk about being high and dry, this was it. We asked so many people if we could stay with them and their responses were either nice or straight to the point – No.

We moved in with Greg's cousin, but that did not work out. Her and her infant stayed there but her mom paid for half of the rent and all the food. She was willing to share some of the food because she had so much, and she was afraid it would spoil before she could cook it. So, we did. Her mom somehow caught wind of the arrangement and cussed us out. She said her daughter didn't pay for crap so she had no say on what we could eat.

We tried local churches from time to time to pick up donated food. Rent demands kept increasing past the initial amount we agreed on, so we had to leave away from there. Next, we went to my aunt's house to look around. At first, she said we could move in with her but then changed her mind when she realized we weren't married yet. She did not want our example of an unwedded relationship to influence her small children. I could not understand then but respect it now.

Next, we tried an old girlfriend from the liquor store that I knew. She was always nice to us when we came in to get our vodka and cognac. We agreed on a rental amount, we bought our own groceries, and we were hardly there due to work and school. She offered to cook us a nice dinner–steak and potatoes. We told her we were cool, but she said it would hurt her feelings if we did not eat her cooking. So, we sat down and ate.

As the days went by, things started to become more competitive. If we bought something they did too. If we didn't share, we would hear her mouth. One time I had driven her and her boyfriend to their appointments. After the appointment, I bought chicken for everyone. I left out one item for her boyfriend (a cup of ice) and she thought I'd done it intentionally. I just didn't want to buy a single cup of ice but would rather buy a bag of ice for everyone.

The room she rented out to us was supposed to be private but that changed too. It was no longer private because she would frequently come through the curtain whenever she wanted to because it was her house or to play with my nose to wake me up out of sleep. Her and her guy would start arguing out of nowhere.

One time I went outside to smoke and here he comes too. She called him to come upstairs but he didn't answer. Finally, she yelled at him, and he ran up the stairs. I heard her yelling at him, "So you going to smoke outside with that woman and won't answer me when I call?" I felt so awkward but even more so when she followed her last statement with this, "I'm the only sinner in this house!"

Shortly after this incident, her boyfriend relapsed and went back to smoking crack and the arguments worsened. They both became violent with one another. The day she threw an iron at him, we felt like two sticks being tossed around by trying to control a big pregnant woman and an angry crackhead. They had previously lost everything, including her grandmother, in a housefire. But her boyfriend, flipped out and told her he was going to burn the whole house down. I told him our grandmothers' pictures were in there, but he didn't care at all. Between that and the sewage waste closing in on us, we decided it was time for us to go.

As we were leaving, her oldest son yelled at her, "Mom, why are you treating them like this when they have been nothing but nice to us? You know how it felt when we were out on the streets or staying with folks." She was so angry she yelled back at her son, "You can go live with them then!" Since we had nowhere to go, we talked him down a bit and called my uncle.

When he picked us up, we told him about all the chaos, and he agreed to let us move in with him. My Uncle is a really busy man working for the city, but he is old school, so I knew we had to play everything by the book. We filled his house with groceries and his comment was, "Now I don't have nowhere to put my stuff." We kind of laughed it off. There were missteps that we tried to abide by, but it was difficult. My uncle didn't like crumbs in the sink when I did dishes, and a feud started when Greg ate a can of soup, he thought I had bought. We tried our best to do what he said because it was his house and we had to respect it no matter what.

Because of our pre-marital counseling, Greg and I were celibate. It was hard to maintain our personal frictions. The smallest thing was nerve wrecking and I got into arguments with Uncle Jay. We packed up before he got home. He called me the next day and said someone broke into his car and stole his radio. We felt like it was karma.

No matter who we lived with it was always something, so we decided to move out to Buckhead and temporarily reside in the parking lot of the mall outside my college door entry. The train station was across the street so Greg could just catch it to work. I continued earning my degree and doing work-study for money.

Under the work-study program I started assisting the corporate staff and one of the department chairs made a joke about homeless people that offended me. I told her that I was homeless, and she said, "Wow! Teaira, I had no idea. You are different. You are a good worker." I took it with a grain of salt but felt proud of myself for sticking up for us 'homeless' people. I never heard them joke about the less fortunate again.

One day at school, God put extended-stay on my mind, so I picked up the phone book at school and began calling around. I had never heard of it before, but it was just what we needed. We moved into a motel on Fulton Industrial Blvd. in Atlanta. No more waiting for the culinary department to cook meatballs for us (the leftovers were dinner from the culinary class saved for us.) No more watching my fellow classmates and mall employees go home at night and clock in, in the morning because we have our own place now. Roaches, prostitutes, and strippers–you name it, but it was ours.

We bombed the room with pesticides, bleached it down and bought air fresheners so it slowly became habitable. One day we were in the bed at about 3 A.M. we hear screaming from the next room." The security officer opened our doors while we were in bed half dressed. She apologized and went back to her guard shack. Here we go again.

Fast-forward a bit, we had finished our premarital sessions and we went ahead and got married. I had a beautiful white dress with an extended train. Greg wore a pinstriped suit. There were only five family members at the wedding and a couple of my friends. It didn't matter to us; the most important people were there and that was Greg and I.

I was nervous and so pressed for time that I forgot the ring and Greg had left his jacket. We straightened things out and marched down the aisle to a song called, "Fly like a Bird." We said our vows. I pretended to put a ring on Greg's finger, we exchanged kisses, said "I do" and had a big party afterward. The only bad thing that happened on this day was when a heavyset lady stepped on Greg's shoes at the after party. He was in so much pain in his already too tight shoes! When I asked him what happened, he said, "That lady stepped on my feet! My toes are already beating like heart beats." That was the laugh of the night.

After the party, we rushed up the stairs to our room and my groom unwrapped his gift! After almost a year of being celibate, it was on and popping! Our experience was not to be compared to any other sexual experience that I had with anyone else because we were Mr. and Mrs. Curry baby with a capital C. We woke up the next morning to our relatives knocking on our motel room door saying that they had tried to contact us, but we would not answer the phone. Here's some advice: never give your family the hotel room number you are occupying on your honeymoon night!

Greg:

So now things are getting serious. I'm in a committed relationship and we are in a one room extended stay in the hood. But we are fine because we felt we had a place to sleep, and we could be ourselves. We're attending church on a regular basis now. One mistake we made before getting married though rested in our last premarital session. Mrs. and Mr. Hill asked us if there was anything else that may have been an issue in our engagement, and we swiftly said 'no.' But I knew deep down inside that was a lie. I knew that the alcohol consumption should have been addressed but I was just ready to finish up those classes. However, to my surprise Pastor Dollar's marriage ministry also offered marriage counseling after getting married as well as before. At first, I thought it would be a waste of time, but it was the best thing ever. This additional bonus helped us out big time.

Our counselors gave us the best advice on marriage. For an example, being all the way open with one another and they even taught us the importance of following God's plan on understanding what marriage is all about and what the purpose is as well.

At First, I thought it meant we could have sex and not be penalized by God. But it was so much more than that. I learned that for marriage to work, you must fully serve your wife and in return she has to serve you as well. I was lost at that point and didn't understand what I was getting myself into. Then the counselor asked, "Are you two living together and having sexual relations?"

We looked at each other and knew where this was going. I answered, "Yeah." Following that session, we began practicing abstinence. This was the test of all tests seeing as we were already having sex and had to stop cold turkey…Whew! We held on for almost a full year until we got married. It was the hardest thing but at the same time it was the most rewarding as well. I had all this energy built up inside of me, so I was able to do very well at work and I slowly started to see how blessed we were while staying committed to the abstinence plan.

There was a time when there was extensive rain and flooding. Everywhere around us flooded except where we were staying. We saw the water going down the street like a river, but it never affected us. We believe God showed us favor because we were obeying His rules for relationships. Not to mention we were clearly living in the hood which normally experienced nighttime fights and drug deals, but those actions *stopped, and it became peaceful around us.*

Before I knew it, the time had come. We were getting married! A friend of mine was set to be the best man. He was much older than me and much wiser as well. Instead of the normal bachelor party, we decided to go shoot some pool and he made a promise to get me to the church on time for the big day. I stayed the night at his house because I wasn't supposed to see the bride until I got in front of the altar. We grabbed a quick breakfast and then went to the church. I was there with the wedding planner, and she literally did everything. Thank you.

I started thinking to myself, what am I doing? Teaira was running late, and she had an important piece that went to my suit, so I was half-dressed. I had too much time on my hands. I wanted to smoke so bad but couldn't because I was on the church grounds. My mind was racing a million miles an hour. Soon after, my bride shows up and everything jumps back into perspective. I am about to get married! Standing in front of the minister, looking back at my mother and family on the other side, I felt a rush of heat go through my body as we began. Considering everything we had been through; we were finally getting to be adults and live our lives together.

Everyone had fun at the after party and I even ran into a coworker at the club. He was a chef and as we took shots, he told me he had been with his wife since high school. He said no matter what you do take care of home first. I took that to heart because I heard that a lot. After a few rounds, and dance sessions, I was ready to consummate the marriage, so we soon left the party. As we continued home it was time to unwrap my gift–my bride.

Going forward, I got sick and thought that maybe I ate something bad. I was at work and still feeling funny. One of the cooks was old school and she made the best buttermilk chicken ever! She told me, "Yep, you are going through the motions. You got her pregnant, didn't you?" I had the symptoms, so I put two and two together, but my wife refused to believe me about the pregnancy until we went to a theme park. She got on a ride and could barely walk after we got off. I just looked at her and smiled because she realized I was right.

After the test came back showing we were expecting I said to myself we can't have a baby here at this extended stay. So, we moved to a better place with no shootings, no loud fights and best of all out of the hood. I had to take care of home as I was told.

Everything was going good and we had the world in our hands. Nine months had gone by and our first born was home from the hospital. I spent all day making sure everything was perfect for him and my wife. As we were discharged to go home, I felt on top of the world! I have my wife and now I have a son!

Lesson:

A wedding is a beautiful thing indeed, but the real party starts after saying the words, "I Do." There's something about starting a family that makes you want to be your very best! Everyone will ask you when you are going to start your family and we have learned to make sure you are ready before doing so. Just like a wedding, when all of your verbal support (family, friends and loved ones) leaves to live their lives, full responsibility sets in. It becomes your obligation to maintain the upkeep of your new garden of life. As newlyweds and new parents, don't worry so much about if you are doing it correctly. God will become your biggest friend with sound wisdom and direction.

Blessing:

"Don't bargain with God. Be direct. Ask for what you need. This isn't a cat-and-mouse, hide-and-seek game we're in. If your child asks for bread, do you trick him with sawdust? If he asks for fish, do you scare him with a live snake on his plate? As bad as you are, you wouldn't think of such a thing. You're at least decent to your own children. So don't you think the God who conceived you in love will be even better?" ~Matthew 7:7 (The Message)

_____

_____

"After the death of Moses the servant of God, God spoke to Joshua, Moses' assistant: Moses my servant is dead. Get going. Cross this Jordan River, you and all the people. Cross to the country I'm giving to the People of Israel. I'm giving you every square inch of the land you set your foot on–just as I promised Moses. From the wilderness and this Lebanon east to the Great River, the Euphrates River–all the Hittite country–and then west to the Great Sea. It's all yours. All your life, no one will be able to hold out against you. In the same way I was with Moses, I'll be with you. I won't give up on you; I won't leave you. Strength! Courage! You are going to lead this people to inherit the land that I promised to give their ancestors. Give it everything you have, heart and soul. Make sure you carry out The Revelation that Moses commanded you, every bit of it. Don't get off track, either left or right, so as to make sure you get to where you're going. And don't for a minute let this Book of The Revelation be out of mind. Ponder and meditate on it day and night, making sure you practice everything written in it. Then you'll get where you're going; then you'll succeed. Haven't I commanded you? Strength! Courage! Don't be timid; don't get discouraged. God, your God, is with you every step you take." ~Joshua 1:9 (MSG)

_____

_____

"Meanwhile, the moment we get tired in the waiting, God's Spirit is right along side helping us along. If we don't know how or what to pray, it doesn't matter. He does our praying in and for us, making prayer out of our wordless signs, our aching groans. He knows us far better than we know ourselves, knows our pregnant condition, and keeps us present before God. That's why we can be so sure that every detail in our lives of love for God is worked into something good. ~Romans 8:28 (MSG)

_____

_____

Chapter 15

The 'D' word (Outside Influences)

"Struggle is a never-ending process.
Freedom is never really won,
you earn it and win it with every generation."
~ Coretta Scott King

Finally, my family is complete now and I gained a husband! We moved to Union City, and it was just my speed. It was quiet, peaceful, and full of elders. Not to mention it was more affordable and family oriented than the extended stay motel room. As a young married woman with a child, I grew closer to Christ. My first child was the reason why I stopped drinking and smoking because I had no choice if I wanted a healthy baby.

My friends begged me not to get married because they thought I'd forget all about them. I told them that was nonsense because I'm loyal. To keep my word, I spent countless hours on the phone with my friends. I was often on the phone until 4 am at times. Greg worked long hard hours and when he would get home dinner would not be ready, the house was not in the best condition and every time he wanted to make love to me, I told him to wait until I got off the phone. I wasn't rude, I was just helping family and friends through their problems but to him I guess he felt neglected.

After I had the baby, I slipped into a slight touch of postpartum depression. I wasn't doing my hair or choosing to groom my body daily. Greg did not have much of a wife to come home to at this point. He was no longer greeted at the door by his wife but felt we'd become roommates with his baby. So, when I denied him of my wifely physical duties, my sweet precious husband would just roll over on the bed waiting for me to get off the phone and fall asleep.

Looking back on things, his last straw was when he waited for me for a while, and he started staring down at the floor. His back was turn toward me and he went to sleep for the last time waiting for me. My husband had changed, and I did not even see it. I thought I had him on lock but even a lock will change when tampered with. Ladies and gentlemen that was the day that I lost the husband as I once knew him.

Greg:

Now that we were in a smaller town everything should be better, right? My wife and I lived in an area that was a little quieter than what we were accustomed to. She was starting to change and didn't smoke or drink any more. I followed her lead and slowed down as well because it was not the same when just doing it by myself. I felt like this was a good thing, but I wasn't ready to make that type of change just yet. She was on her phone all the time helping people out, giving advice and just keeping up with her friends. The problem was that this left little to no quality time for us. I knew for the most part she was doing what she felt was God's plans for her helping other people out and spreading the word of God to her friends. I couldn't argue with that, so I just waited until she was done. Sometimes she just never got done.

I then met up with someone who lived in the same apartment complex, and we began to hangout. He was cool. We just smoked and talked about whatever was on our minds. Everything was going good. She would be inside the house on her phone, and I would be outside hanging out with my new friend.

Then I met more of his friends, and we started going to clubs and pool halls. We chilled out with the fellas. Between work and hang time, my presence at the house got smaller and smaller to the point where I was going out just to avoid going home. After work I would get some coworkers together and we would go to the bar next door to us. Soon the female workers wanted to go as well because of the talking about all the fun we would have. In my mind, I was thinking that it was all harmless. We work together, might as well chill together. As time goes by, the little crew of six turned into ten and then fifteen as more workers would come along—so did my popularity. And then came the temptations.

When seductively approached, I would brush them off and let them know I'm married and that I don't roll that way. But because my wife was never in the mood for anything and my neighbors constantly needed something from me, the urge to get away was strong. After a few more months of this, I finally broke down. When an old girlfriend back from Minnesota was waiting at a bar I visited for me, I found myself talking about my problems. One night she said, "I'll take you home." After several shots and a few beers, that sounded like a good idea. Next thing I know, I'm going in and out of sleep and ended up at her house.

I felt guilty about it but being ignored at home made it easier to go home with this other woman. It got to the point where I didn't want to go back home to my wife because I was spending time with someone else like me that smoked and drank. And she paid attention to me. One day on my way to work, my wife asked me what I wanted to do with our marriage. I said, I wanted a divorce. I saw her almost in tears, but I didn't feel bad. I wanted the party life and wanted to be single again so I could have more fun. I even started flirting with coworkers and drinking on the job.

One day chilling with the fellas, I started getting weird vibes about where I was at. It seemed like I was *getting too much attention from a lot of people. It's hard to explain but it was the same feeling I felt when I went back to Minnesota because everything just felt wrong (familiar spirits.) I stopped going out so much after that and couldn't figure out what was going on.*

Things started changing at home with my wife. I remember Teaira cooked me dinner even after I'd asked her for a divorce. I thought for sure she had poisoned it! I would ask her, "Why are you doing this?"

She just laughed and said, "Because I love you."

I did not want to eat that food, so I just went to bed. She came in and wanted to talk to me. I said, "Who me? Well, you're not on the phone so…"

She began to tell me that she was sorry. I tried to end the conversation but continued. I told her I was seeing someone else so she might as well stop. Looking back, I was a cold man. She cried and I just went into the living room and slept there.

Teaira:

I wondered, how this could happen when I had him on lock? We had disagreements all the time, but this took the cake! What made this time such an ultimatum? We were 4 ½ months pregnant with our second child and I started having contractions early. My OB thought that I was over-exaggerating until she checked my cervix, and I was already dilated and effaced. So, in the middle of our troubled marriage, I was going to have a premature baby. This was a stressful time for sure. I cried out to the Lord, "Please, let me make it all the way through this pregnancy with this innocent baby girl. Let her dwell inside of me for protection."

I knew Greg's patterns which were pretty simple, but his cycles changed. When I went looking for him at the train station and he wasn't there, the first thing I did was call the hospitals, jails, his job and he wasn't anywhere. When he broke the news to me, feeling sad was an understatement. I thought that I'd become the next statistic in my family to have a broken household with baby daddy drama. When he told me that he wanted out of the marriage, I felt shocked! When your man cheats on you, a million questions run through your mind like: who is she and where can I find her?

Things continuously changed in the Curry household, but one thing remained the same; it was just me, my unborn, and my imagination of what he was out there doing in the streets. I called Greg every day and now suddenly, I had all the time in the world for my man. One night he came home drunk blasting music and told me to stay in my room.

I worked hard to try to be the "obedient and submissive" wife that Christians talk about. I was told, just do everything he says Teaira even if he's not in his right mind because a wife MUST be submissive at all times. Deep down I knew something was off when he went outside because I was left in the room for over an hour. I tiptoed to the front door and found my husband outside talking to that whore! I ran back in the room filled with tears of disbelief. So, T what's next? Do you get better or even?

At the time my anger wanted me to crush everything in sight. I visualized the other woman and instantly I saw blood and staples all over her body. I also saw I could be having a good time myself with other dudes from around the way. I was told by a couple of men that they loved having sex with pregnant women because their body is extra lubricated. Pregnancy wasn't necessarily something that would stop them from hitting "it" with me. I felt that would be nasty to have another man inside my body with my husband's seed planted and growing inside me. Also, I made a vow before God not to break the covenant that we made with the Creator! I had to fill this void with something though, so I pulled out my spiritual weapons and went to work!

Greg:

For a few weeks she just kept on pouring love into me no matter what I did or said. When we were in the bedroom, I had a nightmare of a strong spirit attacking me. I thought I had woken up, but it was just one bad dream after another inside my bedroom. When I finally did wake up, she asked me, "What's the matter. Let me pray for you."

She held my hand and started praying for me. While I was drunk, I could see shadows on the walls moving around really fast and I told her that she shouldn't pray for me because it would make those spirits angry. I blacked out and woke in the morning.

After that night, I really wanted to know what was going on with me. That search led me to demonic possession and occult practices. I read a lot of books about it and even found some DVD's on the subject. The demon inside of me was constantly being fed by the spiritual consumption of bad fruits. My wife was getting better but for me the nightmares continued to torment me. I got paranoid about everything.

While hanging out in the apartments heavily intoxicated, my wife showed up. She told me to come on in the house because it was our anniversary. I didn't want to leave and my drinking buddy tagged along singing 'it's your anniversary' over and over to irritate Tea. She was so mad because she felt he was tearing our marriage apart. I couldn't see it then because I was lost in my own world.

Very slowly I was waking up to the voice of God. She would pray for me and fast even if I was going out to a party all night. God started working on me big time! Friends started leaving, money started to run dry, parties stopped too. It got to the point where my drinking buddies and I couldn't even afford a beer. Then all the bills started to pile up and it forced me to stay home and see what was really going on as a result of my wrong doings.

My wife continued to be humble and focus on God. I went to church with her, and the spark started to come back into my marriage. I felt the heavy spirits lifting off of me and I began getting myself back together and loving my wife again. I started fasting with her and asking for forgiveness for all the wrongs I had done. As I was trying to get my life back together, bills were still due, and we had to move yet again because we couldn't pay rent. To top it all off, I lost my job that I'd had for years. I had just become a supervisor after eight years but as quick as I got the promotion, it was taken away from me. It was like I was cursed for breaking the covenant we made before God. As a man, I needed an outlet and I needed one fast. I was trying to change but I was still paying for all of the damages I caused. When you make mistakes in your marriage, it affects the whole house, and everyone suffers.

Lessons:

Never assume that when you get married, you have that person on 'lock'. There is no such thing. Your significant other could be rich or poor, weak, or strong and there is a person that will accept them. Sometimes that person will tempt them just to cause discord in your relationship. It is important to remember why you decided to be in a relationship with that person. Pay close attention to each other's needs or someone or maybe even something else will. When evil first presents itself within the marriage, find a way to shut it down immediately.

Blessings:

"If you want favor with both God and man, and a reputation for good judgment and common sense, then trust the Lord completely; don't ever trust yourself. 6 In everything you do, put God first, and he will direct you and crown your efforts with success." ~ Proverbs 3:5-6 (TLB)

_____

_____

"For we are not fighting against people made of flesh and blood, but against persons without bodies— the evil rulers of the unseen world, those mighty satanic beings and great evil princes of darkness who rule this world; and against huge numbers of wicked spirits in the spirit world." ~ Ephesians 6:12 (TLB)

_____

_____

"So give yourselves humbly to God. Resist the devil and he will flee from you." ~ James 4:7 (TLB)

_____

_____

Chapter 16
Taken for Granted

"The kind of beauty I want most is the hard-to-get kind that comes from within
–strength, courage, dignity."
~ Ruby Dee

My marriage was crumbling and at this point I quickly realized I could either stress myself out or I could stick it out. I'd never seen an example of a marriage going through tough times and working it out. No woman in my upbringing had ever fought for their marriage, so I had to learn. I thought that I was going to catch a case, but the spiritual side of me showed me how to use holy weapons to battle with. These weapons were fasting, praying, reading (not only my bible but books that helped me develop my internal strength) and most of all being loving to him in spite of him.

Out of all these actions that I took, love was the most powerful. Loving in a way that Jesus does will make you do the things that are necessary to keep your marriage where it should be. I had become a brand-new woman. Friends and family advised me to give it up and turn him loose but something within me was not ready to let our relationship go. I knew who I had married, and I knew who I had fallen in love with. One thing I did not know was why this and why that. When I started listening to the voice of God, He showed me that I had a huge role to play in the depreciation of our marriage. You should have seen me! I was on a personal mission to find out what I could do to save our marriage.

Many times, we look at the other person's stains, but we overlook the spots of our own lives. One day I said, "Lord I surrender, and I am desperate! Show me, oh God, what am I doing wrong or what do I need to do more of?" I completely surrendered my thoughts, my actions, and my marriage over to the Great Creator! That was my war cry and my plea. I asked God to show me what I could do to bring my husband back and the first thing He did was show me a vivid reflection of myself. It played inside my head like a movie. I could see all the times I denied him sex, just to be on the phone with other people. The times he was actually working overtime so I could be a typical stay-at-home wife, but I didn't perform my wifely duties.

God showed me Greg was coming home looking for dinner but instead found a cold stove. After work when he opened the front door, he was not greeted by his Queen instead, he was greeted by his nappy haired, non-showered, dirty house, problem solving for every other household other than his own part-time wife. You may say that I am coming down on myself a little too harsh, but it is what it is, and I had to woman up and accept my faults. If you're not showing love and affection to your spouse, you have become a roommate with a court ordered title. Playing that Shero for others but neglecting the very one that I took vows with is chaotic.

What is a vow? A vow is a solid promise made to someone and unfortunately my vows became conditional depending upon who needed me first. Now don't get me wrong, I did not mean any harm but that's exactly what happened. Before I can continue with the rest of my story, let me tell you ladies something: NEVER put anything or anyone before your marriage!

OK, back to the juice!

Being on a computer was a hobby for me, so I believe that God used what I enjoyed the most to help me find a solution. I typed in the YouTube search bar "Marriage Testimonies", and I began to watch like I've never watched before. I saw scenarios that were worse off than mine and I saw some that were better. One marriage was crazy! The husband and his wife had separated but they remained in the same house. The wife stayed on her side of the house bawling her eyes out every time he ushered in a new hot date! I said to myself "Wow! That could never be me!" But out of all the testimonies I saw, one stuck out to me the most. The woman who cared for everyone else but her own hard-working hubby. She was known as the neighborhood shero because she cooked meals for the neighborhood kids, had people over for dinner, cleaned clothes for others, etc. Her husband would come home from work, and he would barely get a hello, so he confided in another woman. That story spoke volumes to me but the part that really resonated with me was when she put God last. She did not even have time for Him! Once that happened, everything else crumbled.

That's why I said I left my husband at the altar and brought home a roommate. The next thing I did was go back to World Changers Church and contacted my pre-marriage counselors. They told me it would be more effective if Greg could come out too, but I responded, "How can I get this man to come? He clearly has changed and is not interested in saving our marriage." Mr. and Mrs. Hill (our counselors) told me to keep on trying to get him to come anyway. So, after asking him a few times and getting blown off, I decided to take him up there without forewarning him. He was mad but he went! The Hills undoubtedly have the favor of God over their lives. They counseled us, prayed with us and we felt an immediate change in our lives. We felt God!

They had a spiritual strategy for us. Over the phone the wife spoke words of encouragement to me, and her husband talked to Greg. Another thing I did was purchased a nice journal. It was very pretty so I wrote every time I felt the urge to do so. The good, the bad and the ugly truth was inside that book, and it created an outlet for me. I could let my true feelings out and keep track of the progress at hand. I bought a book on marriage for wives only by Mr. Tony Evans. I also found a daily devotional/gratitude book and every day I read a different gratitude piece. This book had exercises you could do to remind yourself of how much God loves us or the fact of how we already have so much to be grateful for. Gratitude is truly the seed for more.

I stopped taking so many calls over the phone and I made sure my house was clean and my body. I bought a wig for those days that I didn't feel like installing a sew in. Other days I just made sure my hair was nice and neat even if it was just a basic ponytail. By this time some more of our problems had leaked out to family and close friends. As his wife I made sure not to let anyone curse my husband with words because he was still my King! When it came down to sex, I made sure that I opened up and became available to him. I stopped making up excuses as to why I could not perform. I also tried new things with him. I was out of my comfort zone on some things but was willing to try it out anyway. I slipped back into drinking and smoking to do what the other woman he had spent time with was willing to do. But I quickly learned never to compromise your relationship with anyone. Even if it is with your spouse, if it is outside the will of God, then not even with your spouse.

I did the best that I could considering my high-risk pregnancy. We communicated more and I was able to tell him when I needed to slow down or what have you. We spoke with the doctor, and I listened to my body to continue satisfying my man and protect our baby.

When we first got together, we watched porn for ideas and excitement, but I came across EX cutters, then EX porn stars and I stumbled across Danielle William's video. I saw her testimony along with others and discovered that some of the girls were abused on set (even during breaks). Some females were not enjoying their roles, and some were even abused verbally. I abruptly closed the door on porn. I felt as if I had learned enough tricks to get the party started on my own.

This part of my marriage taught me to look at self initially. We always try to blame the other person but nine times out of ten, YOU too could have also done something differently to extinguish the flame that creates the fire. Things were becoming normal again until…

Lessons:

Be careful who you invite inside of your marriage circle. If you need to vent, talk to someone who is pro marriage. Sometimes our loved ones that are single just don't understand the responsibility of being in a marital covenant with God. It's also helpful if they believe in God as well. I say that because some things are spiritual and there will come a point where you need the power of God to come through on the behalf of your marriage. Gossiping about the problem to family and friends can sometimes stir up more strife. So don't be afraid to communicate with a counselor or therapist of some sort. Don't know of any? Trust me, when you seek, you will find. Don't give up!

Blessings:

" ...and let us consider how to encourage one another in love and good deeds..."

~ Hebrews 10:24 (NASB)

_____

_____

"Above all, love each other deeply, because love covers over a multitude of sins."

~1 Peter 4:8 (NIV)

_____

_____

"Do not let any unwholesome talk come out of your mouths, but only what is good for edification according to the need of the moment, say that, so that it will give grace to those who hear."

~ Ephesians 4:29 (NIV)

_____

_____

Chapter 17

Inner Demons

*"We need to do a better job of putting ourselves
higher on our own 'to do' list."*
~Michelle Obama

Teaira:

We had moved into a spacious apartment over in Jonesboro, Georgia and we had given birth to our first baby girl! No more infidelity, no more late nights wondering where he was. I catered to him daily and he did the same for me. It felt as though we were in the honeymoon stages all over again because we were attracted to one another and showing each other what love really was.

However, I will never forget this one night as long as I live; One night I could not stay asleep because Greg was not beside me. I got up looking for him and he was outside on the patio in the pouring rain with no shirt on sitting Indian style with a can of beer in his hand. I called him a few times and finally he came into the house. I said, "Baby come on into the room and get some rest."

He came in and laid down beside me and said, "Baby, please pray for me, I need prayer." As tired as I was, I did a quick prayer in hopes we could catch some Z's. He stopped me and said, "No, I need some serious prayer baby."

I shook off my fatigue, looked at him and I could tell he was serious. I put my flesh to the side and filled up the atmosphere as a complete prayer warrior that was ready for war! Out of nowhere he started spazzing out! He hit the wall with his fist and left a huge hole. Then he went back into prayer mode. His hand hit the wall several more times while yelling obscene things. His voice changed into a weird creepy tone, so I knew I was dealing with strong demonic forces. He stopped again to pray, and I told him to open his mouth and boldly call on Jesus! All he could say repeatedly was, "The blood of Jesus!"

One more time he went out of character and this time he grabbed a butcher knife in the kitchen. I was shocked but knew I had no room for fear. God allowed me to safely get the knife from him and threw it away from us. I don't know how but he was completely naked trying to walk out of the front door with a weapon. I stopped him. I knew the devil wanted him to kill himself or someone else to off him out of fear if he walked out the door. I called my First Lady to pray around 2 AM and when she heard the commotion, she asked me to call the cops. About 12 police cars showed up and took him straight to the hospital. It was hard for me to see them rough him up, but they safely transported him directly to the hospital.

Greg:

As everything was getting better, I started drinking heavily again but this time by myself. That night my wife is referring to is when I drank seven cans of strong beer and was sitting on the patio out in the rain shirtless. I drank so much beer to where I didn't feel drunk at all! I was totally sober again, or so I thought. Keeping my cool, my wife asked me to come in and I told her to let me finish my drink. That was my problem, I couldn't stop till all the drinks were gone. She prayed deeply for me. My wife has never prayed so hard for me. On the other hand, I was going in and out as if I were in a pool and I would go underwater. Everything was blurry, my hearing was muffled and then I would pop back up and I could see and hear again. Next thing I knew I was in a padded room where several police and doctors had to pin me down. They finally gave me a shot to calm me down. When they left the room, I could hear them talking. Thick white foam bubbled out of my mouth. One of the doctors said, "This is impossible, Mr. Curry has received two cocktail shots and he should be out by now!" Meanwhile, I was still calling on Jesus and spitting up. Then after what seemed like forever, I finally closed my eyes and woke up in the bed with my wife sitting next to me. It was amazing to me that even through all that, she was still right there by my side.

Teaira:

Greg was released from the hospital and his family wanted to see him. Some people were still trying to offer him strong drinks. I was so proud of him for turning down everything. I could not understand why people would offer him something that put him in the hospital. Sometime after that, my brother fell on hard times and asked us if we could allow him and his girlfriend to move in with us. We allowed it. Remember, hubby had lost his job, so he was filling out applications day and night. Real men do not feel good when they can't provide for their families so to relieve the pressure, he would play video games after diligently coming home from looking for work. My brother's girlfriend only saw him playing the game and tells me he needed to be doing more to take care of us. I was shocked! We had never charged them rent

84

and we watched her child on numerous occasions for free to help her get on her feet. I did not feel it was her place to tell me her opinion. She did not know the whole story. She had to go.

*Never let others ruin your marriage especially if they don't have a pot or a window.

Once we let go of our excess baggage, Greg had finally gotten a new job! We started going to church again. A guy from the church started coming over to our house to work on creating our very first single that I wrote. Greg and he produced the music and things were smoother than suede at this point. Shortly after producing the track, a radio DJ had me come down to the radio station for an interview, while playing the new song that I wrote.

Egos started forming due to the producer's wife wanting a reality show out of the deal. She wanted fame plus she was so tired of him staying over our house working on CD's that she had threatened to stab him at our studio session! We agreed it was a done deal and so was the music. Once again, we've reached stagnation in our first break but by the same token nothing could stop us now. We did it before we could do it again. To succeed we had to release all the excess drama and baggage.

Lessons:

Pray over your spouse regardless of what you see. If things are good–pray. If things are bad–pray even more. Also be mindful of returning to your own vomit because backtracking creates a stronger stench. Those family members that tried to get Greg to take a drink could have made matters worse. Even to the point of death this time. Once you get back on track, leave the old negative mindset behind you for good and watch those blessings begin to flow into your life. Standing up for what's right may involve stepping away from those that may unknowingly cause harm.

Blessings:

"Therefore, what God has joined together, let no person separate." ~Mark 10:9 (NIV)

_____

_____

"So they are no longer two, but one flesh. There for what God has joined together, no person is to separate." ~Matthew 19:6 (NIV)

_____

_____

"Nevertheless, as for you individually, each husband is to love his own wife the same as himself, and the wife must see to it that she respects her husband." ~ Ephesians 5:33 (NASB)

_____

_____

Chapter 18
Spiritual Warfare (Postpartum)

I grew tired of our family being under the radar, so I decided to take a real estate class for our progression. I completed the class, took the course but failed the test and never went back to retake it. We were pregnant with child number four now and when I had her, I had the worst case of postpartum depression ever! It lasted so long the doctor said that at a certain point it just becomes regular depression. Our precious baby girl was laying between me, and Greg and her eyes started glowing. I saw shadows in the room, and I was terrified to go to sleep to avoid the treacherous torture nightmares. While awake I was petrified of what I might see. I woke Greg up and we prayed together hard. Together we decided that I needed the medication the doctor offered me because at this point, prayer alone was not penetrating to the core for me or at least it seemed that way. Even though I had a C-section, family and friends were pulling on me for favors which I lifelessly agreed to.

There was a Pastor I reached out to from the television. He had me doing weird stuff to pair with the items he sent to me through the mail. One day, he sent out a circular piece of paper in the mail. His instructions were to tear the paper into four pieces and place them in each corner of my room and we would receive a blessing. Another time he advised me to wear his 'special' bracelet. Things got worse in my mind. Nothing he prophesied came to pass so indeed this was a witchcraft manipulation. I hurriedly left his ministry alone.

And once again, I slipped back into smoking weed and the munchies were no joke! With the depression I gained 51 pounds. I was huge and out of breath standing at a hefty 251 pounds. I felt so unattractive. "What a big fat failure you are Teaira" was the voice I heard in my head.

Greg:

I noticed my wife was watching a lot of negative shows involving murder, death or just eerie stories so I told her she might want to chill with that. She snapped back, "This is my outlet, just let me watch my shows!"

One day she was watching the most uncanny show on the planet. I immediately took the phone from her, took the battery out as well and told her, "You are not watching that!" I noticed she was in fear of everything. I could feel it in the house every time I stepped in from work. She would be sad and say, "I'm fat," she would just come down on herself hard. I had to put a stop to that with extra love by complimenting her, communicating more with her and a lot of praying too.

*As the man of the house, you must be aware of the energy in your home. Pay attention to what your wife or kids may be going through. You need to work on the issue the moment you see that something is wrong.

Teaira:

Greg's actions really helped out a lot! I know that it's a handful for a man to do a full shift at work and then come home to a spiritual mess, but my husband really helped out my healing process by watching over the ways of the house. Something I should have been doing but could not move toward the light. I was held captive in mental and spiritual bondage at the time. Life began to get back to normal for me. One day I looked in the mirror and decided enough was enough. No more negative movie binges feeding the depression, no more smoking weed. This new way of thinking even helped me with my weight loss journey. I just claimed, No MORE!

I started my weight loss journey and in looking for diets, I found a healthier lifestyle. I would read my Bible. For joy, I'd go to the book of Psalms. For wisdom I'd go to the book of Proverbs. Finally, I could see the light again!

Lessons:

Postpartum depression is real. Ladies, after having a baby it is important to monitor how you feel. If you are still depressed after a few weeks of having your child, seek help as soon as you can! You are not less of a person if you need to, get professional help or medication. Bring God into everything but also use wisdom. Gentlemen, pay attention to your woman and try to maintain a joyful atmosphere paired with love. Women go through a lot of hormonal changes after having a baby. You can do things like playing their favorite songs, having date nights, telling her how much you still love her, etc. Signs of depression may include her staying in bed all day, isolation from things that previously spiked her interest, as well as crying sporadic tears. The list goes on, but you will know if your woman's energy has shifted. Prayer, monitoring what I watched, getting sunshine, counseling, and anti-depression medication helped out a lot! That and my husband playing his part as well by showing compassion amongst other things.

Blessings:

"But Jesus often withdrew to lonely places and prayed." ~ Luke 5:16 (NIV)

_____

_____

"Do you not know that your bodies are temples of the Holy Spirit, who is in you, whom you have received from God? You are not your own; you were bought at a price. Therefore, honor God with your bodies." ~ 1 Corinthians 6:19-20 (NIV)

_____

_____

"Don't you know that you yourselves are God's temple and that God's Spirit dwells in your midst? If anyone destroys God's temple, God will destroy that person; for God's temple is sacred, and you together are that temple." ~ 1 Corinthians 3:16-17 (NIV)

_____

_____

Chapter 19

God's Glory

Once our lease was up, we moved to a more privileged area. No more bus lines and no more hearing domestic violence between the walls at night. Our children went to a charter school, and it proved to be a better environment than the public schools. This new school had so many extracurricular activities for them, and they were happy. I could not have been happier.

Finally, peace and quiet. A beautiful park with a book nook to read and return books too, a water pad play area, and exercise machines were also located inside the park. Upon signing the lease with an option to buy we blessed our new home, anointed it with oil and blessed each room. It was a 35-minute commute to get Greg to his job, but we made it work until our minivan broke down. We had a nice neighbor that let us use her car for a while. I had to drop off my neighbor to work, then take Greg to work, pick her up, then she would in return pick him back up. We paid her weekly for her troubles.

I had just written my first book called "Fed Up? Change Up!" which catapulted me into being a business owner, motivational speaker and Life Coach. That book is a product of a rape that I overcame along with the dismissal of HPV. Not to mention the countless relationships I was involved in before sealing the deal with Greg. I had a conference that I was asked to speak at, and I asked my neighbor if I could pay her to take me.

When I asked her, I could feel her growing tired of me even though we paid her $320 a month. It was her car, and she was tired of us disrupting her flow. That morning she reluctantly took me to the event, and I remember going into the bathroom first to cry, then centered myself to be able to encourage the people and deliver a message that could change their lives. Long story short: I did my thing at that event in spite of!

That next morning, I got a call from a dealership to come check out a new car. They picked up my family from the house with their shuttle van and off to the dealership we went. After going through their screening process, a few hours later, we had our very first brand new car. It only had eight miles on it, zero money down, 45 days no payments, and someone inside the dealership paid our first month's insurance too. You can't tell me God isn't good!

I continued to get to requests to speak at different venues and my brand began to grow. The invitations grew and so did my number of viewers for my online inspirational videos. Finally, I put my business degree to use, and Greg stayed on his job to secure the bills. My husband started to participate with me when I ministered to God's people, and do you know how good that felt to see something I prayed for coming into fruition? Still to this day, I am very proud of who my husband has become spiritually, physically, and mentally. Everything we do or say in our marriage is a seed, so we watch what we say, what we do and how we do it.

I consider myself to be very blessed to have Greg as my husband because I realized all those hardships did nothing but make our love grow deeper and stronger for one another, so you get the gist.

Greg:

After all these years of mistakes and trials, we finally get to a place of understanding and peace. My wife and I withstood many blows to our marriage, but we still held on to one another and didn't let go! All the fruits of our labor were starting to show up in our lives now. We had to disconnect with the world and plug into what God wanted us to do. For example, when the van broke down, we eventually decided to just give it all to God.

For a while, it would seem like we would face hard times yet again, but we decided we were able to look at the situation and smile. We understand that God had something better in store for us. Our mental and spiritual strength grew to a point that we trusted God would come through for us once again. He initially provided our blessing in the form of a neighbor by providing temporary transportation for us.

By remaining happy, it wasn't long before we were blessed with a brand-new car, and we knew God was on the move. It wasn't what we received but how we had received it. I found joy in coming home from work listening to my wife's innovative plans about generating our new business Fed Up/Change Up!

Ideas of me working behind the cameras and my wife working in front of the cameras started forming. I began moving forward and realized that our testimonies could help someone in their times of need.

My wife and I are proof marriage is challenging but you get out of it what you put into it. As I am studying the word of God with my wife, together we agree on things and head toward the new beginning of our lives. As we grow in God, we grow more in love with one another. We also grew in the understanding of life, marriage, parenting and how to treat people. Our marriage has a good purpose which is why I feel we are a team working together to better one another and now to help others as well.

Greg and Teaira

As we close, we would like to leave you with this thought: What does "Changed Up! Now What" really mean?

Marriage is the great change everyone fantasizes about. But what you do after the vows are set and everyone goes home makes the difference of a long marriage. After the honeymoon is over, and the sex becomes a regular thing, now what? What do you do when the babies come into play and rearrange your entire life around the art of parenthood? Lastly, how do you react when your spouse gets on your last nerve as time goes by? Now what? Do we call our mothers? File for the big D and return to dating? Do we walk out because our partner is failing from health issues or addiction? The answer is NO! As long as abuse is not in the picture, our commitment is to do all that we can to sustain our marriages because it is a three-way covenant between both spouses and God.

Often, we can get so excited about the thrills inside of the wedding we forget to invest in the lifetime involved within the marriage. To all the married couples out there, we trust you have learned from our lessons. You know our motto, "My lessons- your blessings!"

For the singles, we don't want to discourage you because marriage can be a beautiful thing, but before you change up, think about the now, beyond dating, and what you can do to build a lifelong solid marriage.

Greg:

Looking back and reflecting on where we were and what we went through. It's amazing to think about. When I was single, I found her phone number in the back pocket of my blue pair of jeans after a break. I can truly say what God has for you is for you! I love my wife and kids dearly and the road we traveled to get to this point was crazy to say the least. I have my faults and so does she. Things in the past were not always visible at times.

When we first got married, I had no clue what I was doing or where to start. I was doing what I felt was right or what TV said marriage should be. I don't blame her for my mistakes. In fact, I am blessed to have been forgiven and I learned from them rather than repeat them. I learned through time I had to change myself for my marriage to change and was mostly by watching my wife's transformation.

I loved her enough to make some changes within myself and together we learned how things should operate in a union. It's still a work in progress and a testament of God's grace over our lives. Lastly, the same thing He did for us, He can do for you!

Teaira:

I must admit when I first got married, I unknowingly took some of the things Greg did for me for granted. I thought getting married would be my saving grace and that was all I had to do. I also felt I had Greg in the palm of my hands. Nobody else would want to date the slim guy I married. I had everything under control! I kept things right in the bedroom, I cook on occasion, and gave the man a baby. He's not going nowhere. Lies, I tell you these are lies we're often told.

I felt there was no need to continue doing what I initially had done to reel him in when I had him on lock. If that's your perception of marriage, I've got news for you—it won't last. You must work to maintain a healthy marriage. We sometimes look at marriage as the end but it's the complete opposite. It's really the beginning of a new life, on a new journey with your soulmate, with your partner for life. Never marry someone with the mindset they are not going anywhere because you believe you have them on lock.

The enemy is always seeking whom he can devour. Someone will come by and fill up the areas you left empty. Let's set the record straight; I do not excuse my husband's affair, nor do I excuse the part I provoked by being neglectful. As a wife, privileged to stay home, I should have tended to our home, our meals, my health, my postpartum depression, and my obesity. I should have gotten the help I needed sooner instead of pretending I had it all together. I needed to first help myself before trying to play savior to the imperfections of others. Some may beg to differ and say it wasn't my fault and that I'm old fashioned, but I know what our home needed.

There must be a level of maintaining the foundation between marriage partners to build a foundation or your precious marriage will fall to pieces. Love, respect, expectation, understanding and selflessness should all be communicated upon before vows are exchanged.

I want to leave you with the most important rule of all; if you keep God in the middle of your marriage, your relationship may bend but it won't break. God is the nucleus that holds it all together.

"I was built this way for a reason, so I'm going to use it." ~ Simone Biles

Lessons:

The closer each person draws to the Lord, the closer you draw to each other.

There are 3 kinds of love: 1) I'll love you if, 2) I'll love you when, and 3) I'll love you in spite of. I'll love you in spite of is the only one that lasts a lifetime.

Blessings:

"Let your fountain be blessed and rejoice in the wife of your youth. Like a doe and a graceful mountain goat, let her breasts satisfy you at all times; be exhilarated always with her love." ~Proverbs 5:18-19 (NIV)

_____

_____

"Seek the Lord and His strength; seek His face continually." ~1Chronicles 16:11 (KJV)

_____

_____

"Therefore, a man shall leave his father and mother and hold fast to his wife, and the two shall become one flesh." ~Ephesians 5:31 ~Genesis 2:24 (KJV)

_____

_____

*Disclaimer *

Domestic Violence and Dating Abuse

If you are being abused in your marriage or your dating relationships – GET HELP IMMEDIATELY! Do not stay in a relationship that causes physical or mental abuse or injury. The National Domestic Abuse Hotline is available 24/7 to assist male and female victims of abuse. Every case is different, but they do offer a range of resources from legal assistance, transportation (getting you picked up and taking you to safety) and verbal support. The web address is www.thehotline.org or call 1-800-799-7233. Know that you are a gem that should be covered in love and protection not blood, bruises and mental stress.

Learn about the Aspire App. Here are some links:

https://www.drphil.com/videos/learn-about-the-aspire-app-and-how-it-can-help-victims-of-domestic-violence/

YouTube video on The Aspire App for Help for Domestic Violence Victims

Here's the Aspire free app: https://www.whengeorgiasmiled.org/aspire-news-app/

Every state has a Domestic Abuse Shelter, look for it online or ask a police officer.

Have an escape plan to get away from domestic violence:

You need to have an escape plan to get away from abuse.

1. Ask for help.

2. Have a code word you can use with someone you can trust that understands that you are in danger and need out now.

3. Start putting money away in a secret place. Place it somewhere you can get a hold of it easily if you need to run.

4. Pack a bag for you and your children that you can also stash somewhere secret. Don't include

your young children in this process so they won't be able to talk about it. Include extra meds, underwear, pj's, change of clothing, duplicate of a favorite toy, grooming items and a treat or small gift (for distracting in the event you must run), a book, crayons, etc. Pack your bible or download the bible app on your phone.

5. Set up some place to go ahead of time. Perhaps a friend or relative that no one knows where they live, or a shelter.

6. Keep your gas tank full in case you need to leave in a hurry.

7. If you must leave, turn your phone off or turn off the GPS tracking so you aren't followed by your abuser.

8. Memorize emergency numbers in case you don't have your phone.

9. While still living with your abuser, create believable excuses to get out of the house so when you must leave, they've heard the reason before.

10. Plan an escape route from your home to a safe place.

11. Make copies of important documents and keep them in a safe place away from your home. You may need them once you leave.

12. Open a bank account in your own name.

13. Make a copy of important keys and give them to your safe person.

Do you know Christ?

If you'd like to, read on:

We are all promised eternal life, the question is where will we spend it? If Heaven is real, so is hell. The good news is, we get to choose.

Want to know Jesus?

If you do not know Jesus as your Savior, begin today. Below are the Biblical reasons to know Jesus.

1). Man's Problem: God loves you so much that he wants you to have an abundant life. We are sinful and that sin separates us from eternal life and knowing God intimately. Man's problem:

a. John 10:10 - The thief comes only to steal and kill and destroy; I have come that they may have life and have it to the full.

b. Romans 3:23 - for all have sinned and fall short of the glory of God

c. Romans 6:23 - For the wages of sin is death, but the gift of God is eternal life in Christ Jesus our Lord.

2). God's Solution: He sent his son to die in place of our sins.

a. Romans 5:8 - But God demonstrates his own love for us in this: While we were still sinners, Christ died for us.

b. John 3:16 - For God so loved the world that he gave his one and only Son, that whoever believes in him shall not perish but have eternal life.

c. 1 Corinthians 15:3-6 - For what I received I passed on to you as of first

Importance: that Christ died for our sins according to the Scriptures, that he was buried, that he was raised on the third day according to the Scriptures, and that he appeared to Cephas, and then to the Twelve. After that, he appeared to more than five hundred of the brothers and sisters at the same time, most of whom are still living, though some have fallen asleep.

3). Our Part: We must each accept our sin, and God's provision for it by receiving Christ as our Savior.

a. John 1:12 - Jesus answered, "I am the way and the truth and the life. No one comes to the

Father except through me."

  b. Romans 10:9 If you declare with your mouth, "Jesus is Lord," and believe in your heart that God raised him from the dead, you will be saved.

  c. Ephesians 2:8,9 - For it is by grace you have been saved, through faith—and this is not from yourselves, it is the gift of God– not by works, so that no one can boast.

  d. John 3:1-8 - Now there was a Pharisee, a man named Nicodemus who was a member of the Jewish ruling council. He came to Jesus at night and said, "Rabbi, we know that you are a teacher who has come from God. For no one could perform the signs you are doing if God were not with him." Jesus replied, "Very truly I tell you, no one can see the kingdom of God unless they are born again."

4). God's Promise: Once we have made that commitment, God's promise to us is that our sins have been washed clean, we receive the Holy Spirit within our hearts, and we are promised to spend eternity in Heaven with Him.

  a. 1 John 5:11-12 - And this is the testimony: God has given us eternal life, and this life is in his Son. Whoever has the Son has life; whoever does not have the Son of God does not have life.

  b. John 14:21 - Whoever has my commands and keeps them is the one who loves me. The one who loves me will be loved by my Father, and I too will love themand show myself to them.

5). Celebrate! Assurance:

  a. Revelations 3:20 - Here I am! I stand at the door and knock. If anyone hears my voice and opens the door, I will come in and eat with that person, and they with me.

  b. Colossians 1:27 - To them God has chosen to make known among the Gentiles the glorious riches of this mystery, which is Christ in you, the hope of glory.

  c. John 5:24 - Very truly I tell you, whoever hears my word and believes him who sent me has eternal life and will not be judged but has crossed over from death to life.

  d. 2 Corinthians 5:17 - Therefore, if anyone is in Christ, the new creation has come: The old has gone, the new is here!

  e. 1 Thessalonians 5:18 - give thanks in all circumstances; for this is God's will for you in Christ Jesus.

Here's a simple prayer to invite Christ into your life:

Dear God, I recognize that I'm a sinner and that sin keeps me from sharing eternity with you. I believe that you died on the cross and took all my sins upon yourself so I would not have to. Please forgive me and come into my heart to rule my life. I believe you have forgiven my sins; past, present, and future, allowing me to be bound to you with the promise of heaven following my death. Thank you for coming into my heart and ruling my life.

Amen.

If you just prayed this prayer for the first time—welcome to the kingdom!

What are Coach Tea and Greg up to now?

Check out our Sunday night 'Let's Talk' call in at https://cu-nw.com/cunw-support-group

Visit our website: cu-nw.com

Join our email list, get weekly tips, discounts and stay on top of where and when Teaira and Greg are speaking!

Subscribe at: https://cu-nw.com/contact

CHANGED UP! NOW WHAT? LLC

1954 Airport Road #1331 Atlanta GA 30341

678-653-2770

ChangedUpNowWhat@GMAIL.COM

CPSIA information can be obtained
at www.ICGtesting.com
Printed in the USA
BVHW030846130722
642019BV00014B/249